Writing Strands

TEACHING COMPANION

Getting the most out of
the *Writing Strands* program.

MASTER BOOKS CURRICULUM

Master Books Creative Team:

Editors:
Craig Froman
Becki Dudley

Design: Terry White

Cover Design: Diana Bogardus

Copy Editors:
Judy Lewis
Willow Meek

Curriculum Review:
Kristen Pratt
Laura Welch
Diana Bogardus

First printing: September 2017
Seventh printing: February 2021

Master Books®, P.O. Box 726, Green Forest, AR 72638

Master Books® is a division of the New Leaf Publishing Group, Inc.

ISBN: 978-1-68344-093-2
ISBN: 978-1-61458-632-6 (digital)

Printed in the United States of America

Please visit our website for other great titles:
www.masterbooks.com

About the Author

Since 1988, the *Writing Strands* series by **Dave Marks** has been helping homeschooling students develop their writing and communication skills. Dave was the founder of the National Writing Institute. He graduated from Western Michigan University, then received a master of arts degree from Central Michigan University. Dave retired after 30 years of teaching writing at all levels, from elementary school through the college level.

Contents

Writing Strands Teaching Companion, Part 1, demonstrates to teachers how to provide supportive and effective feedback on writing assignments. It includes information on common conditions that make teaching composition difficult and on common writing problems, examples of feedback on real assignments, explanations of drafting, and spelling rules. This information is essential to those working with the *Writing Strands* series, but anyone responsible for providing feedback on written works would benefit from this book as well.

Throughout its levels, the series organizes writing into four strands: creative, argumentative, report and research, and expository writing. Success with the four strands of writing is contingent on how well students understand the following foundational skills, which are taught in the lower levels of *Writing Strands*: creative, basic, organizational, and descriptive writing. Once the students have mastered these fundamental skills, they are ready to apply them to the abstract subject matter of the upper-level books. The books introduce students to the mechanics of writing: syntax, spelling, punctuation, and grammar. These elements are taught experientially and over time as the student works through the writing exercises. Many students thrive with this type of experiential learning; however, some students may need additional instruction or a more methodical approach to grammar. If so, we recommend incorporating *Language Lessons for a Living Education* and/or the *Jensen's Grammar Bundle* into their curriculum plan, both by Master Books.

Students in grade 9 and above will earn 1 language arts credit for each level of *Writing Strands*.

Writing Strands Teaching Companion, Part 2 focuses on understanding and evaluating literature. An overarching premise of Writing Strands is that "good readers make good writers." The reading half of any language arts program should involve reading and talking about books and ideas and this section provides extra guidance to get the most out of the reading week.

One of the goals at Master Books is to help students develop critical thinking skills. In that light, students are encouraged to answer the same questions about each piece of literature they read at each level. This is intentional and designed to help them think about what they read. We want these questions to become second nature as they progress through life and encounter literature from various sources. It is okay if your student cannot answer all of the questions each week, but you should see a progression in their ability to analyze what they are reading. In a culture where words are used to influence worldview, it is vital that we are able to analyze what we read in order to understand the truth or application.

The *Reading Strands* components of each level have a specific focus on one aspect of literature and the first five books in the series use character-building Bible stories and other biblical texts to illustrate these points. For the most part, these stories all focus on the same biblical characters each year. Sometimes, students will revisit the same story multiple times, always analyzing it from a different angle, while other times they will read stories from different times in these characters' lives.

Flexible Grade Level Recommendations:

Beginning 1:	Grades 5–8
Beginning 2:	Grades 5–8
Intermediate 1:	Grades 6–9 (1 credit hour for 9th grade)
Intermediate 2:	Grades 6–9 (1 credit hour for 9th grade)
Advanced 1:	Grades 7–10 (1 credit hour)
Advanced 2:	Grades 7–10 (1 credit hour)

Overview of Series

Writing Strands Beginning 1 focuses on aspects of literary characters while *Beginning 2* teaches students all about literary setting. *Intermediate 1* introduces students to the elements of literary plot, and *Intermediate 2*'s literature lessons are devoted to learning about literary elements, such as point of view, literary devices, and genre. *Advanced 1* then introduces students to an in-depth study of figurative language. *Advanced 2* has students apply all the literary analysis aspects they have learned as they work their way through John Bunyan's classic *The Pilgrim's Progress*.

In the **Appendices** section you will find information on teaching vocabulary with English word roots, spelling rules, a listing of biblical genres, a basic listing of literature genres, commonly confused words, a section on grammar terms, a glossary of the literary terms used throughout Writing Strands, and the *Writing Strands* Scope and Sequence. This section will be helpful to you at different times as you teach through the levels of *Writing Strands*.

Part 1: Writing Strands
Teaching and Evaluating Writing

Helping Students Write

There are some things that students need that you can give them. They need to feel good about what they do. Making your students feel good about learning to write is not hard to do. When they write, they put their hearts on a page; they want to learn and to please. As a teacher, you are in a great position. Find something wonderful in what the student has written and ask him or her to read it aloud because you think it is so beautiful. Now the student will feel good about what has been written. At this point, rather than point out all the things that are wrong with the paper, you can show one or two ways to make it even better. Focus on **only one or two** at a time to avoid overwhelming the student. Read that one rule and explain how it works. Help the student apply that rule to the writing. This will demonstrate how that application will improve that sentence. Now, read it again and compliment the student on the sentence! Your students will be encouraged because of your praise and also because your feedback is not just devoted to listing lots of errors.

If you take this approach, your students will look forward to writing; they will not be afraid of making mistakes; they will learn the rules as they apply them to their writing; and they will feel good about what they are learning. The most important benefit of all is that they will learn to love their language.

Issues that Make Teaching Writing Hard

Fear and insecurity are the two conditions that are the most damaging to writing competence.

What you need is a program of instruction that is appropriate for each child's skill level, that has easy-to-follow steps, and that leads to the production of essays, reports, descriptions, and pieces of fiction. With such a program, you can help children become competent writers. *Writing Strands* is such a program and gives you the resources to help your students succeed at writing. If you follow the advice in this book, you will transmit confidence to your students, and you will convince them that they can learn to write well.

Lack of motivation is a problem for some children. They do not see the importance of writing. All it takes is ten minutes every day. If children see adults sit down with books for ten minutes each day and that they let nothing interfere with their "reading time," the children will soon accept the value of words on paper. A student who is eager to learn to read will be just as eager to learn to write. Giving your students a love of reading and writing is of great value.

Lack of concentration is a problem for many children. If the problems with concentration are not clinical, there are some things you can do to help. Concentration is greatly aided by focus. The child needs to know what to do, how to do it, where to do it, when to do it, and that it is possible to do it. The lessons show the student what to do and how to do it. You must provide the "where to do it, when to do it" and convince the child that it is "possible to do it." If you give each child a time and a place to write that is distraction free and you show him that you have confidence in his ability, then it will be possible for him to concentrate for the short periods of time necessary to do the daily work in *Writing Strands* lessons.

Trouble with thinking through ideas and how to present them is a problem for many young writers. The lessons in *Writing Strands* solve this for you by showing your students how to do each assignment. The lessons in *Writing Strands* have been designed to help the students think through the process of producing each paper.

Mechanical problems exist for all writers, but talking about them with your students need not be the most stressful time of the day. The important thing to keep in mind is that your students will be with you for years. They will get frustrated if you point out everything they do that is wrong. Pick one mechanical problem each week and let the rest slide. The next week pick another one and let the rest slide. Soon you will have covered the major issues without all the frustration.

Trouble with following directions is a big problem with many young writers. Have your students read their assignment and then tell you what they think they will be doing. Then ask them how they plan to start. If they seem to have any trouble, clarify any misunderstandings, go over the directions to see exactly what they state, and then form a plan on how to start. Give lots of congratulations and praise. They need confidence that they can follow directions.

Resistance to writing is not uncommon. It can help a student if the instructor responds, "Done already? You sure must be good at this writing stuff. I'm so proud of what you have done. Read that sentence to me. I think it is beautiful." Even if you need to search very hard for something nice to say about your student's writing, it is important to do so. Say good things and then find one thing that, if changed, might make the writing even better. Remember — address one thing each week (or longer, if necessary). Your student wants to please you, and if you praise his writing, he will want to write.

Reluctance to rewrite is understandable, especially for young writers. Rewriting is a lot of work. If you approach rough drafts as just that, rough, and allow them to remain rough (your students will recognize this), then cleaning them up will not be such a big job.

A rough draft should have lots of problems in it. It is not supposed to be pretty, and the spelling is not supposed to be perfect. There should be cross-outs and missed periods. It is just getting ideas down on paper. It is your students' thoughts on paper about the subject. Give your students a chance to correct all the problems before you comment on them.

A word processing program is a wonderful thing for students to use for writing. It makes rewriting so easy since they can make changes without rewriting the whole paper. If your students are frustrated with the rewriting process, consider letting them write on a computer.

Trouble with proofreading is easy to understand. After all, proofreading is hard to do well. It takes practice, but there are some things you can do to help. Have your students read their papers aloud to you. Your students will hear mistakes when they read aloud that they will miss when reading to themselves. If they do not catch the mistakes, you read to them from their papers. While reading aloud, care should be taken that they read exactly what is on the paper. We all have the tendency to read what we should have written and not the exact words that are there. You might have to read over their shoulders to make sure of this, but it is worth it. They will pick up the habit of proofreading aloud and thus catch many of their own mistakes.

Rules for Drafting and Formatting

To learn to communicate, students need to have goals, an audience, and a person more adept than they are at word use who can look at their efforts and advise ways to improve them. That is where drafting comes in.

If we give students writing assignments, collect them, write comments on them, grade them, and return them, many students will learn nothing about writing. If writing training is carried on this way, many students will write on the second paper the same way they wrote on the first. They might look at the corrections the teacher made on the first paper, but that is all. They will continue to make the same errors and will have no opportunity to develop the writing skills they so desperately need.

First Rough Draft

There should be a point to any writing experience. It does not help a child to say to him, "Write anything at all. Just give me a page or two on anything you are thinking." That would be hard for anyone to do. For the first draft, students need to concentrate on developing their ideas and explaining them effectively and clearly. We should not look at that first draft and comment about anything other than the big-picture aspects of the paper, such as organization, content, and clarity. Do not worry about spelling or periods or uppercase letters or commas. That comes just before the final draft.

Now is the time to compliment the child on his thinking. "I can see you have thought about this subject some. Did this occur to you? How about this? I like your thinking here, nice touch. What a wonderful idea you had at this point. I sure would like to see more about that."

After reading the first draft, you should give the student directions for further explorations of his ideas. Try to provide general comments about the flavor of his work, encouragement to re-examine his thinking, or new avenues of thought that might produce what you feel should be explored in the exercise.

As long as the student is trying to do as the directions indicate, your comments at this point should all be positive and very supportive.

Second Rough Draft

The student has taken your encouragement and advice and rewritten his first draft. Now there should be some form to the writing. You should be able to tell whether the student is doing as the directions suggest. The directions in *Writing Strands* are very explicit, and you should expect the student to follow them, or you can change them and have the student follow yours. In either case, you should see in the second draft how the student is producing writing consistent with the objectives listed at the beginning of each exercise.

This draft is where you can look for the details that will produce a well-written third rough draft or final draft. Now check for the ideas as they flow through the sentences. Look for paragraphing. Make suggestions about redundancies and awkward phrases. Mention accidental rhyming and check for clichés. This is the kind of help your student needs at this point. If you see that the assignment is brief enough to not need more than three drafts, suggest that your student check the spelling and punctuation before the final copy is written.

Final Copy or Draft

After the student has rewritten the second draft using your suggestions, you should ask to see it before it is turned in to you as completed. If the student wants to take the chance on using ink, that is no problem. You should be able to catch little problems and point them out in this last draft. If you feel it is important that you have a finished paper to keep on file, then you can ask that the paper be written in ink. This version should be polished.

Remember, nobody can write a perfect paper. However, as students learn to write, they can substantially improve. Keep a list in your *Writing Strands* book (or a separate notebook) of the problems that you and your student will solve in the future. They cannot all be solved this week. It will be hard, but it is important that you have patience with misuse of apostrophes until you get to them. One problem solved each week will, in two years, produce quality writing.

Formatting

In most university classes, the instructors will tell the students what style sheet to use for the papers done for each class. If this isn't done, the university library will have style sheets recommended by the various departments.

For *Writing Strands* exercises, we recommend some formatting to get the student in the habit of following these types of directions. This will also help your student's work look tidier over the years.

1. Your student's full name should be in the upper left corner of the paper. Under that should be the assignment title or number. Under that should be the date. This information should only appear on the first page.

2. There should be a title with the major words capitalized on the first line of the paper. The title should never be underlined unless the words are also the title of a book. Then there should be one skipped line before the body of the paper.

3. The top, side, and bottom margins should all be the same size. This is usually one inch. Paper final drafts of papers written after the eighth grade should be double spaced and typed if possible. Only white paper should be used, and only one side should be written on.

4. In the Advanced levels, students will be writing papers that are typically longer than one page. Therefore, page numbers should be added. (Note: Teacher, there are various style manuals that give different formats for numbering pages. It is up to you to decide how your students should format their page numbers.) There should never be the words The End written at the end of any paper or story.

How to Correct Problems in Spelling

In *Writing Strands* there are pages for you to keep track of your student's spelling problems. We recommend that you make each of your students an expert at the spelling of only one word or pattern a week. If this word or pattern is pulled from their writing (a word they have chosen to use), then they will see that word as important to them and necessary to their writing. They will understand that learning to spell that word (or pattern) is relevant.

Next week (or whenever your student has mastered last week's word) pick another relevant word or pattern from a writing exercise and have your student become an expert in the new words or patterns. In this way, in a few years, your students will have good vocabularies they use that they can spell, and you will have eliminated the anxiety and failure with memorizing and testing of spelling lists. Research shows that learning spelling words in abstract lists stays with a child only until the test and then is lost. Only short-term memory is used in such exercises. The average adult in this country has a spelling vocabulary of about 300 words. Do not expect young children to have too much more than that.

Spelling rules can be found in the Appendices.

How to Correct Problems in Writing

There are some very important things to keep in mind when working with children and their writing:

1. All of us need to feel good about what we do. Students must feel good about their attempts to write. Every time your students write, find something wonderful about it. Locate the best phrases, expressions, sentences, paragraphs, or ideas and talk to them about how well they are expressed. Have the student read these wonderful words to you. Have them read them to someone else. Have them read them to the class. Discuss why they were written as they were. Enjoy the beauty of the words with them. Your students will be more ready to write next time and share their work with you.

2. You cannot correct all problems with one paper or all problems this week or this month, or even this year. If you find everything that is wrong with every paper, your students will soon become discouraged.

3. Mechanical and stylistic problems are best solved on a need-to-know basis. Pick one or two problems a week at most to work on. For example, one week work on apostrophe use for contractions, the next week work on apostrophe use for possession, and the next week work on another, and so on.

Important Terms and Common Problems

Ambiguity

An ambiguous statement may be taken in more than one way.

She saw the man walking down the street.

This can mean

    A. She saw the man as she was walking down the street.
    B. She saw the man who was walking down the street.

Often, a sentence is ambiguous because a pronoun (it, she, they, them) does not have a clear antecedent (what it refers to).

Bill looked at the coach when he got the money.

This can mean

    A. When Bill got the money, he looked at the coach.

    B. When the coach got the money, Bill looked at him.

Ambiguous statements should be rewritten so that the meaning is clear to the reader.

Apostrophe

An apostrophe (') is a mark used to indicate possession or contraction. Rules:

1. To form the possessive case (who owns it) of a singular noun (one person or thing), add an apostrophe and an *s*.

   Examples: *the girl's coat*   *James's ball*   *the car's tire*

2. To form the possessive case of a plural noun (two or more people or things) ending in *s*, add only the apostrophe.

   Examples: *the boys' car*   *the cars' headlights*

3. Do not use an apostrophe for *his, hers, its, ours, yours, theirs, whose.*

   Examples: *The car was theirs.*   *The school must teach its students.*

4. Indefinite pronouns (could be anyone), such as *one, everyone, everybody*, require an apostrophe and an *s* to show possession.

   Examples: *One's car is important.*   *That must be somebody's bat.*

5. An apostrophe shows where letters have been omitted in a contraction (making one word out of two). Note that the apostrophe goes in the word where the letter or letters have been left out.

   Examples: *can't* for *cannot*   *don't* for *do not*
               we've for *we have*   *doesn't* for *does not*

6. Use an apostrophe and an *s* to make the plural of letters, numbers, and of words referred to as words.

   Examples: *There are three b's and two m's in that sentence.*
               Do not say so many "and so's" when you explain things.

Audience

Writers do not just write. They write to specific readers in specific forms for specific purposes. To be effective, writers must decide what form is most appropriate for their intended readers so that they can accomplish their purposes.

Keep in mind that just as your students talk differently to different audiences, they must write differently also. They would not talk to you or their minister the same way they would talk to each other or their friends.

As you read your students' writing, think of who their intended audiences are and try to judge how what they are saying will influence those people.

1. Informal — colloquial (used with friends in friendly letters and notes):

   Man, that was such a dumb test. I just flunked it.

2. Semiformal (used in themes, tests, and term papers in school and in letters and articles to businesses and newspapers):

   The test was very hard, so I did not do well.

3. Formal (seldom used by students but appropriate for the most formal of written communication on the highest levels of government, business, or education):

   The six-week's examination was of sufficient scope to challenge the knowledge of the best of the students in the class. Not having adequately prepared for it, he did not demonstrate his true ability.

Awkward Writing

Awkward writing is rough and clumsy. It can be confusing to the reader and make the meaning unclear. Sometimes just the changing of the placement of a word or the changing of a word will clear up the awkwardness.

If you ask your students to read their work out loud or have someone else read it to them and listen to what is read, they can sometimes catch the awkwardness. Remember that they need to read loud enough to hear their own voices.

1. *Each of you will have to bring each day each of the following things: pen, pencil and paper.*

   This should be rewritten to read:

   Each day, bring pens, pencils, and paper.

2. *The bird flew down near the ground and, having done this, began looking for bugs or worms because it was easier to see them down low than it had been when it was flying high in the sky.*

   There are many problems with that sentence. To get rid of its awkwardness, it could be rewritten to read:

   The bird, looking for food, swooped low.

Keep in mind that the point of your students' writing is for them to give their readers information. The simplest way to do this may be the best way.

Cliché

A cliché is a phrase or sentence that has become an overused stereotype. All children like to use expressions they have heard or read. It makes them feel that they are writing like adult authors. You will catch expressions that they do not realize have been used so many times before that they no longer are fresh and exciting for their readers:

pretty as a picture	*tall as a tree*	*snapped back to reality*
stopped in his tracks	*stone cold dead*	*flat on his face*
roared like a lion	*white as a sheet*	*graceful as a swan*
stiff as a board	*limber as a willow*	

Usually the first expressions young writers think of when they write will be clichés. If you think you have heard an expression before, you might suggest they not use it, but help them think of new ways to tell the readers the same information.

Commas

Commas separate ideas and clarify meanings. Teachers often see comma usage as problematic, even though all writers have some comma placement rules they ignore. Keep in mind that children cannot learn all the comma rules at once, and some will never learn them all. To help your students with commas, teach them the basic patterns that require commas. They can then look for these sentence patterns in their own writing.

Rules: Your students should use commas in the following situations:

1. To separate place names — as in addresses, dates, or items in a series

2. To set off introductory or concluding expressions

3. To clarify the parts of a compound sentence

4. To set off transitional or non-restrictive words or expressions in a sentence

Examples:

1. *During the day on May 3, 1989, I began to study.*

   I had courses in English, math, and geography at a little school in Ann Arbor, Michigan.

   The parts of the date should be separated by commas, and the courses in this sentence which come in a list should be separated by commas. Your students have a choice of whether to put a comma before the and just prior to the last item on a list.

2. *After the bad showing on the test, Bill felt he had to study more than he had.*

   A comma sets off the introduction — *After the bad showing on the test* — from the central idea of this sentence — *Bill felt he had to study more.*

3. *Bill went to class to study for the test, and I went to the snack bar to feed the inner beast.*

   There are two complete ideas here: 1) *Bill went to study;* and 2) *I went to eat.* These two ideas can be joined in a compound (two or more things put together) sentence with a comma and a conjunction (and, but, or) between them.

4. *Bob, who didn't really care, made only five points on the test.*

   Notice where the commas are placed in the example above. The idea of this fourth sentence is that Bob made only five points on the test. The information given that he did not care is interesting but not essential to understanding the main idea of the sentence. The commas indicate that the words between them are not essential to the meaning of the sentence.

Comma Splice

A comma splice is when the two halves of a compound sentence are joined/separated by a comma without an appropriate coordinating conjunction (and, or, but).

Example:

   Bill had to take the test over again, he felt sorry he would miss the party.

This comma splice can be avoided by writing this sentence in one of the four following ways:

1. *Bill had to take the test over again and felt sorry he would miss the party.*

2. *Bill had to take the test over again, and he felt sorry he would miss the party.*

3. *Bill had to take the test over again; he felt sorry he would miss the party.*

4. *Bill had to take the test over again. He felt sorry he would miss the party.*

Notice that the punctuation in each of the above examples shows a different relationship between the two ideas. For example, correcting a comma splice by adding a coordinating conjunction and a comma indicates that two ideas are connected much more than separating them with a period does. Using a semicolon to correct a comma splice indicates more of a connection between the ideas than a period would but less of a connection than a comma and coordinating conjunction does.

Dialogue Structure and Punctuation

Dialogue is conversation between two or more people. When shown in writing, it refers to the speech or thoughts of characters.

Rule: Dialogue can occur either in the body of the writing or on a separate line for each new speaker.

Note: Use quotation marks when a character is speaking dialogue. If a character is just thinking something but not saying it aloud, use italics when typing and quotations when writing by hand.

Examples:

1. John took his test paper from the teacher and said to him, "This looks like we'll get to know each other well." The teacher looked surprised and said with a smile, "I hope so."

2. John took his test paper from the teacher and said to him, "This looks like you and I'll get to know each other well."

    The teacher looked surprised and said with a smile, "I hope so."

3. John took his test paper from the teacher and thought, *This looks like I'll get to know this old man well this year.* The teacher looked surprised — as if he had read John's mind — and thought, *I hope so.*

Diction

Diction is the specific selection of words. There are at least four levels of diction:

1. Formal: The words of educated people when they are being serious with each other

    Example: *Our most recent suggestion was the compromise we felt we could make under the present circumstances.*

2. Informal: Polite conversation of people who are relaxed

    Example: *We have given you the best offer we could.*

3. Colloquial: Everyday speech by average people

    Example: *That was the best we could do.*

4. Slang: Ways of talking that are never used in writing except to show characterization in dialogue

    Example: *It's up to you, cook or get outta the kitchen.*

Figurative Language

Figurative language uses what are called figures of speech. A figure of speech describes something in a way that is not literal. The meaning is not exactly what is written. It is figurative or not real. Figurative language can include techniques like personification (assigning human characteristics to non-human things), metaphors (comparisons), similes (differences), and allusion (indirect reference). Figurative language can also use imagery to add deeper meaning (ex. sparkling, creepy, colorful) or even convey sound (ex. buzz, snort, cough).

Example: The murky fog tip-toed through the garden gate, then curled to hug the proud roses. (personification)

Example: The sun danced lightly upon the gentle violets sleeping beneath the posts where the ivy sprawled in lazy joy.

Flowery Writing

Your students will use flowery writing when they want to impress their readers (you) with how many good words they can use to express ideas. This results in the words used becoming more important than the ideas presented.

Rule: A general rule that should apply is: What your students say should be put as simply as possible.

Example:

> *The red and fiery sun slowly settled into the distant hills like some great, billowing sailing ship sinking beyond the horizon. It cast its pink and violet flags along the tops of the clouds where they waved briefly before this ship of light slid beneath the waves of darkness and cast us all, there on the beach, into night.*

This is so flowery that it is hard to read without laughing. It should be rewritten to read:

> *We remained on the beach gazing at the darkening sky while the sun set.*

Fragment

This is part of a sentence that lacks a subject or a verb or both. Check your students' sentences to make sure they have both subjects and verbs. They should avoid using fragments in their expository papers.

Some writers use fragments effectively. Your students may do this in their creative writing. Fragments can be powerful if used correctly:

> *When Janet reached her door, she found it was partly open. A burglar! Someone had been in her house and had left the door open.*

In this example. "A burglar!" is an effective fragment because it helps emphasize Janet's surprise. Unless a student is trying to achieve a specific effect in creative writing, fragments should be avoided.

Modifier (Dangling)

A modifier should be placed as close as possible to what it is modifying so that there is no ambiguity. A dangling modifier is a modifier that is not placed next to what it modifies, which is confusing for the reader.

Examples:

1. *Getting up, my arms felt tired.* (How did the arms get up all by themselves?) This should read: *When I got up, my arms felt tired.*

2. *Coming down the street, my feet wanted to turn into the park.* (Again, how did the feet do this?) This should read: *Coming down the street, I felt as if my feet wanted to turn toward the park.*

3. *Being almost asleep, the accident made me jump.* (It is clear the accident could not have been asleep.) This should read: *I was almost asleep, and the accident made me jump.*

Omitted Words

Children often leave words out of sentences, or they leave the endings off from words. You can help them with this problem if you have them read their work out loud and slowly. Insist that they read slowly so that you can catch every syllable. Depending on the reasons behind the omissions, reading aloud can help your students catch the words they have left out.

Paragraph

A paragraph is a group of sentences that tell about one topic (a topic is the subject or main idea you are telling about). The first sentence of most paragraphs tell the reader what the main idea is, and the rest of the sentences add more details and an ending. Sometimes, a paragraph can be one sentence.

In nonfiction writing, a paragraph consists of a topic sentence and other sentences that support the topic sentence with additional details. A good guideline is that a paragraph in expository writing should have at least four supportive sentences, making at least five sentences for every paragraph.

Paragraphs help organize information in reports, essays, or other forms of writing. A topic sentence is one sentence that introduces the reader to the main idea of the paragraph. Paragraph development may be made by facts, examples, incidents, comparison, contrast, definition, reasons (in the form of arguments), or a combination of methods.

Parallelism

Two or more parts of a sentence or list that have equal importance should be structured in the same way. In a list, the items must be the same part of speech.

Examples:

1. *We went home to eat and reading.*

   This should read: *We went home to eat and to read.* This is obvious in such a short sentence, but this is an easy mistake to make when the sentence is complicated.

2. *There are a number of things that a boy must think about when he is planning to take a bike trip. He must think about checking the air pressure in his tires, putting oil on the chain, making sure the batteries in his light are fresh, and to make sure his brakes work properly.*

   Notice that in this list there is a combination of three parallel participles and one infinitive, which is not parallel in structure. (This sounds like English-teacher talk.) What it means is the first three items on the list (*checking*, *putting*, and *making*) are parallel, but the fourth item on the list (*to make*) is not parallel because it is not structured the same way.

   This sentence should be rewritten to read: *He must think about checking the air pressure in his tires, putting oil on the chain, making sure the batteries in his light are fresh, and making sure his brakes work properly.*

Pronoun Reference and Agreement

To keep writing from being boring, pronouns are often used instead of nouns.

Rule: It must be clear to the reader which noun the pronoun is replacing. The pronoun must agree in case, gender, and number with that noun. The most common error young writers make is with number agreement.

Examples:

1. *Betty and Janet went to the show, but she didn't think it was so good.* (It is not clear which girl did not like the show.)

2. *If a child comes to dinner without clean hands, they must go back to the sink and wash over.* (The word *they* refers to a child, and the number is mixed. This should read: *If children come to dinner without clean hands, they must go back. . . .*)

3. *Both boys took exams but Bob got a higher score on it.* (The pronoun *it* refers to the noun *exams*. The number is mixed here.)

4. *Everybody should go to the show, and they should have their tickets handy.* (The problem here is that the word *everybody* is singular, but the pronouns *they* and *their* are plural.) The following words are singular and they need singular verbs: *everybody, anybody, each, someone.*

Quotation Marks

Quotation marks are used to indicate exact words and to indicate the titles of short works and chapters of long works.

Rules:

1. Your students should put quotation marks around direct quotations (someone's exact words).

    When they use other marks of punctuation with quotation marks, they should put commas and periods inside the quotation marks.

    Other punctuation marks (e.g., question mark, exclamation mark) go inside the quotation marks if they are part of the quotation; if they are not part of the quotation, they go outside the quotation marks.

    Example: *The salesman said, "This is the gum all the kids are chewing."*

    Example: *Is that why he said, "Come here right now"?*

2. Put quotation marks around the titles of chapters, articles, other parts of books or magazines, short poems, short stories, and songs.

    Example:

    In this magazine there were two things I really liked: "The Wind Blows Free" and "Flowers," the poems by the young girl.

Redundancy

Redundancy means using different words to say the same thing. The writer does not gain by this, only confuses and bores the reader.

Examples:

I, myself, feel it is true.

It is plain and clear to see.

In the first sentence, "I" and "myself" means the same thing. The sentence can just be "I feel it is true."

In the second sentence, "plain" and "clear" mean the same thing, so only one of them is needed: "It is plain to see." "It is clear to see."

This is an easy mistake to make, and it will take conscious thought for your students to avoid this problem. You will have to help them find redundancies in their work. There are no exercises they can do that will help. Just have them use care when they are proofreading their work.

Run-On Sentence

This is the combining of two or more sentences as if they were one without appropriate punctuation. Run-on sentences should be fixed by breaking them into multiple sentences or by adding appropriate punctuation (see "Commas").

Example:

Bill saw that the fish was too small he put it back in the lake and then put a fresh worm on his hook.

Any of the ways to fix a comma splice can also fix a run-on sentence. This sentence could be broken into two sentences by putting a period or a semicolon between *small* and *he*. It could also be rewritten to read:

Bill saw that the fish was too small, so he put it back in the lake and put a fresh worm on his hook.

Sentence Variety

Young writers have a tendency to structure all or most of their sentences in the same way. You need to help your students give variety to the structuring of their sentences. A common problem for young writers is that of beginning most sentences with a subject-verb pattern.

Example:

Janet bought a car. The car was blue. It had a good radio. She liked her car and spent a lot of time in it.

These sentences could be re-written and combined so that they all do not start with a subject and verb.

The car Janet bought was blue. Because she liked it so much, she spent a lot of time in it.

Subject-Verb Agreement (Number)

Closely related words have matching forms, and when the forms match, they agree. Subjects and their verbs agree if they both are singular or both are plural.

Rules: Singular subjects require singular verbs, and plural subjects require plural verbs.

Singular:	*car*	*man*	*that*	*she*
Plural:	*cars*	*men*	*those*	*they*
Singular:	*The heater was good.*		*The heater works well.*	
Plural:	*The heaters were good.*		*The heaters work well.*	

Most nouns form their plural by adding the letter *s*, as in *bats* and *cats*. The clue is the final *s*. It is just the opposite with most verbs. A verb ending in *s* is usually singular, as in *puts, yells, is,* and *was*.

Most verbs not ending in *s* are plural, as in *they put, they yell*. The exceptions are verbs used with *I* and singular *you: I put, you put.*

Most problems come when there is a phrase or clause between the subject and the verb. Example:

This red car, which is just one of a whole lot full of cars, is owned by John and Bob.

It is easy for some young writers to think that *cars* is the plural subject and write the sentence this way: *This red car, which is just one of a whole lot full of cars, are owned by John and Bob.* The subject of this sentence (*This red car*) is singular; there are just a lot of words between the subject and the verb, and it confuses the number.

Tense Error

Tense errors occur when past and present tenses are mixed without justification. Rules:

1. Present tense is used to describe actions that are taking place at the time of the telling of the event.

   Example: *John is in the house. Mr. Jones lives there.*

2. Past tense is used to describe actions that have already happened.

   Example: *John was in the house. Mr. Jones lived there.*

3. Future tense is used to describe actions that will happen.

   Example: *John will be in the house. Mr. Jones will live there.*

Transitions

Transitions are bridges from one idea to the next or from one reference to the next or from one section of a paper to the next.

Rule: Writers should use transitions to bridge ideas for their readers by

1. using linking words (*however, moreover, thus,* and *because*) and phrases like *on the other hand, in effect,* and *as an example.*

2. repeating words and phrases used earlier in the writing.

3. referring to points used previously. Examples:

If your student writes two paragraphs about pets, one about a cat and one about a dog, your student should transition between the two paragraphs. Below, the idea of having fun with the cat will help transition to the paragraph about having fun with the dog. *On the other hand* is a transition phrase that helps the reader move between the two ideas.

> *. . .and so I have a lot of fun with my cat.*

> *My dog, on the other hand, is fun for different reasons. We spend time. . .*

Unconscious Repetition

Unconscious repetition will distract the reader, create unnecessarily wordy language, or emphasize parts of a passage that do not need to be emphasized. Conscious repetition is fine so long as it serves a deliberate purpose.

> *To select magazines which are written on the reader's level of reading and interest, a person should select magazines that reflect his economic and intellectual level.*

This could be re-written to read:

> *A person should select magazines to fit his reading ability, interest, and budget.*

Unconscious Rhyming

Unconscious rhyming happens when a writer accidentally uses words that rhyme. The rhyming words will ring in the reader's mind and detract from what the writer wants the reader to think about.

> *The man was feeling really well until he fell.*

The sentence could be re-written to read:

> *The man was feeling really well until he stumbled on the driveway and slid under the greasy truck.*

Voice (Passive and Active)

Most sentences are built on the order of subject-verb-object. This produces an active voice. If a passive verb is used, it inverts this order and makes it seem as if the object were doing rather than receiving the action of the verb.

> Your students' writing will be more forceful if they use active voice.

Examples:

Active:	Bill threw the ball.	We must spend this money.
Passive:	The ball was thrown by Bill.	This money must be spent by us.

Your students can use a passive voice if:

1. The doer of the action is unknown

2. The action needs to be emphasized

3. The receiver of the action is of more importance than the doer of the action.

Examples:

1. *When we were gone, the house was burglarized.* (The person who broke in is unknown.)

2. *No matter how hard they played, the game was lost.* (The game being lost is the most important thing.)

3. *My pet mouse was eaten by that cat.* (The mouse is more important than the cat.)

Wrong Word

The words your students use do not always mean what they think they do.

Rule: Your students should not use words in their writing that they do not use when speaking. If they would never say the words *alas* or *to no avail* or *travail,* they should not write them.

Part 2: Reading Strands
Teaching and Evaluating Literature

Introduction for the Teachers and Students of Reading

This section will help you understand how to discuss fiction with your children. The ideas presented here are based on the knowledge that there can be great joy in reading and that good literature can enrich anyone's life.

Of course, there is value in solitary reading, but the enjoyment that can be found in stories is greater if it can be shared with others. There are models here of conversations with young readers as a way of showing how reading experiences can be enjoyed by both the young readers and their teachers.

Many adults, faced with the challenge of teaching literature, have the feeling that the job is too great to be reasonable. True, it is a daunting enterprise, but it can be an exciting and fun one. A good rule of thumb when teaching students about fiction is that there are no right answers, but there are some definite wrong ones. In literature, there is no one answer to the question of what a text means, though answers to that question needed to be rooted in what the text actually says. For example, a symbol in a text can have several meanings and there is no one right answer for that meaning, though it would be wrong to just say that the symbol represents aliens when there is no other evidence of that in the text.

The important thing to keep in mind is that reading should be fun. If the young reader does not enjoy reading, it may be because reading is seen as work. The reader is either above or below the level of the material, or the material has not been selected with the reader's interests in mind.

Using Reading Strands and the Principles of Teaching Literature

Reading can become a rich and rewarding part of life. Teachers/parents can encourage their children to love it using the following suggestions:

1. A beginning reader must have fun reading. The time spent reading each day should be looked forward to with great eagerness.

2. Young readers must observe, as role models, older children, parents, and teachers enjoying reading. If the new reader sees this going on, there will be a desire to join in this pleasure.

3. Young readers should see their role models talking about what they are reading. They should see them read bits and pieces to each other from a variety of sources.

4. Young readers need to have others show an interest in what they are reading and what this makes them think about.

5. Young readers need to talk about what they have read. This ensures that they think about the ideas in the stories, that they remember the actions, and that they can feel the excitement of sharing the stories with others.

6. When a parent/teacher gives a child a love of books, they give not just the books but the world of ideas. It makes possible adventures and intellectual challenges found in no other place.

Goals and Objectives

Education is a process which changes the learner. If you accept this concept, then you must expect changes to occur in your student's thinking and/or behavior because of your work together. You must decide which changes are possible and which ones are desirable. What do you want your student to "get" from the reading you'll be doing together?

What does your student want? Of course, very young children will not be able to articulate these ideas as you will, but still children will "want," and their desires should be taken into consideration. The goals you establish should be written so that they'll be available to you as you work toward them. It is recommended that you and your student talk about and decide upon these goals together. Your goals may sound something like these:

> Thinks critically, Enjoys reading, Respects other cultures, Appreciates having a quiet time, Appreciates good literature, Develops an interest in history

Specific objectives describe precisely what cognitive outcomes can be expected as a result of the program. The following pages will highlight the outcomes you can expect from this program by age level.

Objectives for Ages Seven and Above

I. **Literal Recognition or Recall** — Literal comprehension begins with the recall of ideas, information, and events in the material read. This would include the recall of:

A. Details: To locate or identify names of characters, the time the story takes place, or the setting

B. Main Ideas: To identify the main idea of a paragraph or a larger portion of reading

C. Sequence: To locate or identify the order of incidents or actions

D. Comparisons: To locate or identify likenesses and differences among characters, places, or events

E. Cause and Effect Relationships: To locate or identify reasons for certain incidents, events, or actions

F. Character Traits: To identify or locate statements about characters that indicate the types of people they are

II. **Inference** — Inferential comprehension is demonstrated by the students when they use a synthesis of the content of a reading, their personal knowledge, their intuition, and their imaginations as a basis for guessing. Have your readers infer (come to conclusions about) the following:

A. Supporting Details: To guess about conditions or situations that the author did not include

B. The Main Idea: To provide the main idea, significance, theme, or moral that is not directly stated in the reading

C. Sequence: To guess what non-stated action might have taken place between two stated actions or incidents or what might have happened before a story begins

D. Comparisons: To recognize likenesses and differences in characters, times, or places that are centered around ideas such as then and now, here and there, or two characters

E. Cause and Effect Relationships: To guess about actions and the resulting consequences

F. Character Motives: To understand the motives of characters based on actions and their interactions with others, and to determine if they are produced by internal or external forces

G. Character Traits: To guess about the nature of characters based on clues presented in the reading

Objectives for Ages Twelve and Above

Older children will come to their reading with a good bit of understanding about how the world works and how they should and can deal with it. You will find that they will react to what they read differently now than they did when they were young. They will come to conclusions that you might not understand or agree with, and you must keep in mind that they are comprehending what they read based on the experiences that they have had. As you work together, you should come to expect and appreciate the differences in how you both understand fiction.

Below are some guidelines for your work with them. You might create your own processes of judging how your readers appreciate their experiences.

I. **Evaluation** — Evaluation is demonstrated by students when they make judgments about the content of a supplied by the parents, authorities on the subject, or by personal experience. These might include worth, suitability, truthfulness, quality, or reasonableness. Evaluation includes:

A. Judgments of Reality or Fantasy: Your students are asked to determine whether events or characters could have existed within the context of the narrative.

B. Judgments of Fact: Your students are asked to decide whether the author has given information that can be supported with facts in the text.

C. Judgments of Worth or Acceptability: Your students are asked to pass judgments on a character's actions. Was the character right or wrong (or good or bad) based on the character's situation and experience?

II. **Appreciation** — Appreciation is how students respond to the selections of language forms, styles, and structures employed within plots, themes, settings, and characters. Appreciation includes:

A. Emotional Response: The student is asked to determine what the author has done to stimulate emotional reactions, such as cheerfulness, happiness, love, hate, fear, tenderness, sentimentality, excitement, suspense, curiosity, boredom, or sadness.

B. Identification with Characters: The student is asked to identify the literary techniques that prompt sympathy or empathy, and what the author has done to make the reader feel like or want to be like a character or not to feel for a character and the position that character is in.

C. Reactions to Language: The student is asked to respond to the author's choice of words in terms of denotation (specific meaning) and connotation (the suggested association or implication) and the influence they have on the intended reader's emotions and thinking. This could include examination of similes and metaphors and their effects.

D. Imagery: The student is asked to recognize the author's ability to create "pictures" with words and to identify what the author has done to engage the reader's sensory imagination.

Selecting Literature to Read

Reading is one of the important steps children take toward becoming adults. The reading they do helps determine the types of people they will grow into. What you select should be determined by the values held by you and that line up with Scripture.

For most children, the fun of reading is dependent on its effects on their ways of thinking. If the reader cannot relate to the character in a story or to the situation that character is in, or if the reader does not care about these things, that reader will not enjoy the narrative. If the young reader can get involved in the lives and situations of the characters, then this experience can be very satisfying.

It is recommended that readers choose at least some of their own books to encourage an interest and love of reading, but some care must be taken in the selection of stories for very young readers and for children who have not yet begun to read. Many reading experts tell us that children need to develop to an extent before they can differentiate between the fantasy of stories and reality. You should choose books that you feel are appropriate for your student and that encourage a biblical worldview.

Many stories have a moral lesson or theme. You should think carefully about this when making selections. The values expressed by books are not lost on young children. It is suggested you examine the viewpoints, value judgments, and stereotypes carefully before you select them for your child.

There are many different types of stories and literature. If you were to walk into your local library and look at the shelves, you would probably find books divided by genre there, with novels, history, cookbooks, poetry, children's books, Westerns, and mysteries, all in different places.

A *genre* is a form of literature in which all works of that type have similarities. For instance, books that are in the Western genre are set in the American West in the 1800s and often feature stories about cowboys, ranchers, and Native Americans. There are thousands of Westerns and none of them are exactly alike, but they still have similar features. A Western would not be set in medieval Europe or be about an ancient king. That would not make sense in the genre.

It is important to know what genre your reading material is. People who are familiar with a genre know what general types of characters, plots, settings, conflicts, and themes to expect because of the genre. For example, mystery readers know that they should expect a story about a crime or something mysterious that needs to be solved, and the focus of the story will be uncovering what happened. Characters will likely include some sort of investigator, as well as suspects and witnesses.

Genres and the Bible

Reading the Bible also requires familiarity with genres. In the Bible, there are historical narratives, laws, books of prophecy, poetry, gospels, and even letters. A historical narrative in the Bible is very different from the Book of Proverbs. The historical passage is going to have characters, a plot, a moral, and is a true account of something that actually happened. Proverbs, meanwhile, have more poetic language and are much shorter. They also teach a moral, but they just state the moral outright. There is not usually a story to follow, and if there is one, it is more abstract than one of the historical narratives.

If you are not familiar with the genres of the Bible, you might find Proverbs confusing until you figure out that it is part of the poetry books. It has a different purpose than the historical narratives, so it also has a different form. There are several ways that genres in the Bible are identified by different books or Bibles by other publishers.

We have included a helpful chart in the back of this book listing the genres and associated books of the Bible that we will use consistently throughout this series.

If you want to learn more about genres of the Bible, we highly recommend Bill Foster's *How the Bible Works* and *How to Read the Bible Literally*. These books both give an excellent breakdown of the genres of the Bible and what to expect in each one. Please be aware that Foster's books are not following the exact genre designations that we are in this course, but they are very informative and easy to read.

Teaching Techniques

The suggested plan for completing the literature lessons is to spend part of each week learning about the literary analysis element being taught, reading the assigned Bible passage, discussing that passage, and completing the recommended activity.

Students should also be assigned a separate book or story to start reading at the beginning of each literature week. At the end of the week, have a literature lesson devoted to the book/story you assigned at the beginning of the week. Weekly lessons, prompts, and activities are included to help you focus on reinforcing the concept taught that week, but it is also important that you discuss the book with them. You will ask questions based on your understanding of the techniques or concepts described, and the student will answer based on their reading and understanding. This method of transmitting ideas is helpful in determining how children are understanding the content of their stories. If their responses leave you confused, you know that they need help in organizing their thoughts.

You will not be teaching children a body of knowledge about literature. You will be teaching them how to extract understanding and meaning from what they read so that they will be able to appreciate literature and benefit from its values for a lifetime of reading.

When teaching very young or beginning readers, the goal is to lead them toward independently being able to construct meaning from the text. The following questions can be used for any reading the student is doing, including the Bible passages in the Reading Strands lessons or books the teacher has assigned.

I. **Prior Knowledge**

  A. Before reading to children, discuss what they already know about the subject. Ask "What do you know about _____?"

  B. Ask your readers to list those points they know for sure are true or which could be true, and those they are not certain about. Discuss this list after the reading.

  C. Have your readers ask prediction questions before the reading based on what they know about a story. As an example: "Our reading today is called *Bob's New Pet*. What kind of a pet do you think it will be?"

  D. Consider prediction questions as you read to them. As for example, "What do you think will happen next?"

E. Ask your readers questions after the reading is over. For example: "What do you think was happening even before this story started?"

F. Ask your readers questions of comparison between the latest book read and prior books read.

II. **Sense Making**

A. Ask children during the reading, "Does this make sense?"

B. Draw from what the children already know about the situations to help them think about them as they read.

C. During the reading, have the children list in their minds likenesses and differences or compare the subject matter with what they already know about it.

III. **Image Visualization**

A. Encourage children to make a picture or a movie in their minds about the topic or story as you read to them.

B. Have children "read" two stories in their minds: one from the words and the other one from the pictures. This is so they can consider similarities and differences.

C. Have the children stop you if you come to new words they are unfamiliar with.

D. Encourage the children to draw pictures of what they hear as you read to them, or they can draw after the story is complete.

E. Use a book that has no words in it and have the children dictate or write the words themselves.

F. As you read to them, have them "draw" in their minds pictures that would go along with the words, then compare their mental "pictures" with the ones in the book.

G. Discuss everything you read to them or that they read themselves. Talk about things the authors did not talk about in the stories, such as the expressions on the faces of the people or what was going on in the next room that the authors did not let anyone "see" into.

Developing Critical Thinking Skills in Very Young and Beginning Readers

The following is a list of some common techniques for helping young children develop the ability to think and analyze what they hear and read. Reading specialists use these techniques as an effective teaching tool.

I. **Recall** — Asking students to tell what just happened in the story. The questions should be specific to a particular event. Recall includes:

A. Details: Student are asked to locate or identify names of characters, the time the story takes place, the setting, or some incident described in the story.

B. Main Ideas: Students are asked to identify the main idea of a paragraph or a larger portion of a reading.

C. Sequence: Students are asked to locate or identify the order of incidents or actions stated in the reading.

D. Comparisons: Students are asked to locate or identify likenesses and differences among characters, places, or events that are compared by the author.

E. Cause and Effect Relationships: Students are asked to locate or identify reasons for certain incidents, events, or actions stated in the reading.

F. Character Traits: Students are asked to identify or locate statements about characters, which help to point out the types of people they are when such statements were made by the author.

II. **Forecasting (predicting)** — Asking students to tell what will happen next. These questions should be preceded by a short review of the immediate events up to that time. "All the kids come to the party except Janet. What do you think will be the reason why Janet doesn't come?" or "The bear comes right into the camp and walks into the tent. Do you think that bear will find the food in the box?"

III. **Inferring** — Asking students to come to conclusions about situations in the story from the information already gained. Inferential comprehension is demonstrated by students when they use a synthesis of the content of a reading, their personal knowledge, intuition, and their imaginations as a basis for guessing. Inferring includes:

A. Supporting Details: Students are asked to guess about additional facts the author might have included that would have made it more informative or interesting.

B. Main Idea: Students are asked to provide the main idea, significance, theme, or moral that is not directly stated in the reading.

C. Sequence: Students are asked to guess as to what non-stated action might have taken place between two stated actions or incidents.

D. Comparisons: Students are asked to come to conclusions about likenesses and differences in characters, times, or places. These are centered around ideas such as then and now, he and she, here and there.

E. Cause and Effect Relationships: Students are asked to guess about the motives of characters and their interactions with others.

F. Character Traits: Students are asked to guess about the nature of characters based on clues presented in the reading.

G. Predicting Outcomes: Students are asked to read the start of a selection and then guess the outcome.

IV. **Personalizing** — Asking students what they might do in the same situation. This might follow a brief discussion of what the character did. "That girl gives her balloon to that little boy who doesn't have one. I wonder why she does that. If you had been that little girl, would you have given him your balloon? If you were in a park and saw a little girl who had a balloon, would you want her to give you her balloon?"

V. **Character Analysis** — Asking students to talk about the actions of a character and asking them to explain why the character did those things. This is a hard one, and you both will need to practice this. "When it is time for the family to get in the car and follow the moving van out of the driveway and to go to their new house, what does Janet do?" (She hid.) "That is a strange thing to do. That would mean that the family would not be able to go. Why would she do that?" (So they couldn't leave.) "Why doesn't she want to leave?" (She would miss her friends.) "What does this tell us about how she feels about her friends?"

VI. **Discussing Values** — Discussing stories gives an excellent opportunity to bring up various values and how they affect our decisions and govern our lives. "When Bob tells John that he had taken the candy from the store and hadn't paid for it, John has a problem, doesn't he? What are the three things he could do? He could tell on Bob or he could try and talk Bob into giving the candy back or paying for it, or he could forget it. What do you think would be the moral, Christian, kind, legal, responsible, proper, necessary, important, or practical thing for John to do?" Thinking through situations like this can help families show how deeply the Bible relates to our daily lives.

VII. **Examining the Resolution (ending)** — Ask students to talk about the ending of the story. This gives them the idea that stories might end in lots of different ways and still be good stories. It stimulates children to think creatively about what has been read. "What do you think about Anne's father stringing fencing around the garden?" (He wanted to keep out the rabbits so they would not eat all the plants.) "What is the purpose of the garden?" (To please Anne. She could not go outside because she was in a wheelchair. She wanted to sit in the window and look at the garden growing.) "Do you like that ending?" (No, I feel sad for the rabbits, and so does Anne.) "Why?" (Because she liked to watch the rabbits eating in the garden.) "Would you like the story to end with the rabbits eating the garden while Anne watched?" (Yes.) "Would you like Anne's father better if he just plants more flowers for the rabbits to eat?"

Extra Help with Meaning for Young and Beginning Readers

It is not uncommon to hear, "I read it again, but I still don't understand." The problem of making meaning (sense) out of a writing is not very easy for us, but for a beginner it is sometimes overwhelming. We all learn things at different rates. If your reader needs extra help, do not worry. The following exercises will help your reader construct meaning from a text because it will help with *the transmission of ideas* in all the categories listed. They are only models, so read through them and decide on specific ideas (words that you would like to use in addition to or in place of those in the examples) to use with your reader.

Analogies

This exercise teaches readers that two words can have the same relationship as two other words. If your reader does not understand how this works, simply wait. Analogies look like these examples:

1. Big is to little as tall is to _____.

2. Full is to empty as fat is to _____.

3. Knife is to cut as pencil is to _____.

4. Cat is to mouse as spider is to _____.

Sometimes the relationships can be very subtle, and some people struggle with them. Other people are very good at seeing relationships, and this is an easy exercise for them. Whichever is the case with your reader, this exercise will help with what words mean and how they relate to each other.

Antonyms

These are words that have opposite meanings. In this exercise, you are to give one word and your young reader is to give a word that means the opposite. This works like this:

1. big — little

2. good — bad

3. light — dark

Cause and Effect

It is important that a reader understand the relationship that words have because one condition causes another. To help your reader see this relationship, you should create a sentence that has a cause and effect relationship in it and have your reader tell you why what happened did happen.

"I forgot to water the plant, and it died."

You are to ask your reader:

"Why did the plant die?"

This seems simple but it can be confusing to a very young reader. What appears obvious to us may be an entirely new experience for a child and not clear at all. Cause and effect relationship can be tricky. Continue to practice this exercise until the student understands the concept.

Classification

This exercise is designed to teach your reader to arrange objects into groups that have similar characteristics. For instance, two- and-four legged animals: "Put the following animals into two groups: one for two-legged animals and one for four-legged animals: chicken, duck, cow, man, mouse, monkey, cat."

As your reader gets older and better at classification, this exercise can become sophisticated. For instance: "Classify the following objects into three groups: airplane, boat, roller skate, ski, trampoline, car, canoe, swing, roller-coaster."

Context Clues

Now that your reader understands that a word might have many meanings, it must be understood how to figure out a reasonable or intended meaning. This can be done by a study of the context (the ideas presented before and after the word). Notice how you can tell the meaning from context in these two examples: "The grocer said he would knock down the price," and "The grocer said he would knock down the price sign." In one instance the words knock down mean to cut or reduce, and in the other they mean to turn over or push over.

In this exercise your reader should learn to determine meaning from context. This should start simply but then make it as complicated as you like. You should write/speak a sentence with a word in it that is not used in its usual way. Your reader then must tell you what the word means in that context.

"Uncle George said he would try and put a good *face* on it."
"Make it look good."

"Bill said he'd *drop* over."
"Come to our house."

"That car is really a *lemon*."
"I don't know. Could it be a yellow car?"

Definition

A good mental exercise for training young readers to understand meanings is to teach them to define words. A good definition has two parts. The first part establishes the general category of the word, and the second part gives some specific information that clearly identifies the object. An example of this is a definition for jackknife. A jackknife is a cutting instrument (general category) small enough to carry in a pocket and has a blade that folds into its handle (two specific characteristics that identify it).

In this exercise, you supply the word and your reader defines it using a two-part definition. Taking turns with this one can be fun. You can have your reader give you a word, and you can define it. Both experiences will help your reader understand words better. You might have to give a good deal of help at first. Examples of this exercise are:

Pickup truck
>   General: truck
>   Specific: small open bed behind cab

Garbage can
>   General: container
>   Specific: designed for trash

Differences and Similarities

The object of this exercise is to help your young reader understand that things/words can be similar and yet be different both at the same time. You are to give two words and your reader is to tell how the two objects or words are different and similar. For example:

1. *Dog* and *Cat*

    Similar: "They both are pets and have four legs."
    Different: "The dog barks, and the cat meows."

2. *Sock* and *Shoe*

    Similar: "They both go on the feet."
    Different: "The sock is cloth, and the shoe is leather."

You could give some variety to this exercise when your reader is ready. You can give the difference and similarity and the category and have your reader name the objects, as in the following example:

3. "The category is clothing."

    Similar: They both cover one end of a person.
    Different: One is worn on the head, and the other is worn on the feet.

    "Hat and Shoes."

Establishing Order

It is important for a reader to understand the order of events in a narration. It seems second nature to us, but it is sometimes not at all clear to a new reader that when a sentence has *after* in it, the event talked about is established in some time frame.

You are to write/speak a sentence that establishes time order (using words like "then," "when," "next," "after," "while," "during," "before"), and your reader is to describe when the event takes place. See the example below:

While the boat burned, we swam to shore.

>   "When did the people swim to shore?"
>   "While the boat was burning."

We went home after we'd eaten dinner.

>   "When did they leave?"
>   "After they'd eaten."

Identifying Categories

We categorize constantly and automatically when we function in our adult lives, but we had to learn to do this. If a person were not to have this skill, each new object he would come across would be in its own category and soon there would be too many categories to keep track. You can help your young reader learn this skill.

You are to list five or six words, and your reader is to tell you which word is not like the others or is in a different category. To do this, your reader will place the words in an appropriate category, and the one that does not fit will be the one identified. This can be done orally or you can write out the lists. It could look like this example:

skate
car
ball
bike
wagon
bus

Your reader will recognize a category that five of these objects will fit into, understand that the sixth one does not fit, and then identify that category. In this case the category could be means of transportation. Your reader might say it like this: "They all are ways to get somewhere except the ball, and that is a toy."

You will have to be careful with this. It could go this way:

"They are all the same. They all roll on the ground, so they are all in the same category."

Meaning

To the very young beginning reader, any word seems like it must mean a specific thing, but we know that most words have a variety of meanings, depending on how and in what context they are used. It will help your reader if you work together, and three or four times a week, you list all the meanings you can think of and find for a word. A good dictionary and an encyclopedia will help.

As a model for this exercise, let's examine the word *plate*. To a young child it might have just one meaning; it is what we eat our food from. This exercise will force you both to examine the meanings of words.

Plate can mean many things:

clutch plate, as in a car;

collection plate, as in church;

book plate, as in publishing;

page plate, as in printing;

gold or silver plate, as in jewelry;

home plate, as in baseball;

blue plate special, as in a diner;

plate-full, as in being very busy;

what's on the plate, as in a business meeting;

a plate, as in a whole course of food at dinner;

a plate, as in a horizontal timber laid on a foundation to receive the wall;

plate of beef, as in a thin slice of brisket;

plating, as in paper making to give high gloss;

plate, as in any sheet of metal.

Wow! Such a variety of meanings gives any young reader an expanded image of the meaning of this word. If a child's understanding of the word *plate* is limited to that from which we eat our food, then much of the meaning in some writing may be lost.

When you first begin this exercise, you will be directive (decide what words to examine and how this is to be done), but soon your reader will want to help you select words. This can turn out to be a word treasure hunt. Have fun with it.

Part/Whole Relationship

You give the two words, and your reader tells you their relationship. The point is to give your reader practice understanding the relationships between parts and wholes. Your student will work to understand the relationships that words have, describe, or establish. Some words describe a part of another word that describes an object. Have fun working on this exercise!

1. *motor — car*

   A motor is part of a car, so this relationship is part to whole.

2. *car — bus*

   A car is a whole and a bus is a whole, so this relationship is whole to whole.

3. *motor — tire*

   A motor is a part of a car and a tire is part of a car, so this relationship is part to part.

This can get confusing, and you should not let your reader get stuck in details unless it is fun. For instance, *piston* is part and motor is *whole*, so in some situations, *motor* is part, and in others it is whole.

To do this exercise, you need name only the objects or their relationships, and your reader can complete the exercise by naming either the relationships or the objects. Of course, if you were to name the relationships and were to ask your reader to name the objects, you would have to name a category for the objects. This would work like this: "I will name a category and you will name the objects. Remember, I will tell you if the relationship is part to part, whole to whole, or part to whole. You will tell me the names of two objects that have that relationship."

"The category for this first game is *car* and the relationship is part to part. What are the objects?"

"*Motor* and *tire*." (These could have been any two parts.)

"Good for you. Now I will name two objects and you are to tell me the relationship. *Pan* and *kettle*."

"Whole to whole."

"How about *pan* and *lid*?"

"Whole to part."

"Right! And what if the category is *animal* and the relationship is whole to whole?"

"*Cat* and *chicken*."

If your young reader does not understand the rules for this game/exercise, wait for six months, and try again. It is better to wait a bit than to frustrate. Keep in mind that this should be fun.

Recognizing Related Words

Words are related in different ways. They may have similar characteristics, like a *rake* and a *shovel* — they both have long handles. They may be used for similar jobs, like a *comb* and a *brush*. They might be associated because of what they represent, like *cooking* and *dinner*.

You are to make a list of words, each followed by four or five other words, and your young reader is to tell you which of the following words is in some way related to the first word. Here is an example:

1. *car — swing, football, bus, table, dog*

2. *nest — ticket, bed, dinner, home, hammer*

3. *bird — snow, feet, worm, horse, phone*

If in number two your reader said *nest* is like *bed*, then your reader has created a category that includes both *bed* and *nest*. For baby birds and children, this is a logical category. If your reader were to make the category to include all birds and all people, then *nest* and *home* would be in the same category. If there is any logic at all to the categorization, then that is the kind of thinking about words you are trying to promote.

Semantics

Now it gets complicated for the young reader. Words mean different things when they are in combination with other words. The combination brings to mind images (connotations) that are different for different people. Even though there are general (cultural) connotations for words, each of us has developed our own personal connotations dependent upon our experiences. These feelings about words, when they are influenced by the context of their use, give us our various understandings about what authors have in mind.

To help you understand how words in combination with other words take on different meanings, examine the words *old man*. Think of the situations and the ways to describe an old man, giving these two words very different connotations and thus giving us different feelings about them. There is the description of grandpa as a *nice old man*. There is *old man Christmas*. There is *old man time*. Death sometimes is referred as *the old man*. A tennis player at 26 is often considered an old man. A boxer is an old man at 30. In the 1960s, a man over 30 was considered an old man. There are kind, nasty, bearded, tired, lonely, and homeless old men. Each of these bring to mind experiences we have had with the concept. The words that surround *old man* dictate how we feel about the old man in question and give different meanings to different people.

To help your student with this concept, you might create a situation and then describe it so it establishes the meaning for the agreed-upon words. To use words like *old man*, you might create the situation (surrounding words) and have your student describe what the words *old man* in that situation mean. Your student will want to change roles with you in this exercise.

Another example is the two words *near* and *far*. In understanding what these words mean, it is important to know what words surround them. Think of how confusing the following could be to a young reader. The kitten crawled *far* from its mother. The moon is *near* Earth. It is *far* to the sun. All of the stars in our galaxy are *near* each other. It is too *far* to ride your bike to the store. The store is too *near* for Dad to take the car. Germany is *far* from here. Summer is *near*. Discussing the connotation of words will help students gain the most meaning from their literature.

Synonyms

Another way to teach meaning is to have your young reader identify whether objects have similar meanings or if the meanings are different. List orally or on paper a group of objects. Your young reader is to identify whether they are similar or not. Here is an example:

> "I am going to give you two words. You are to tell me if the words mean the same thing to you or not. Remember, there is no way you can be wrong in this because I asked you to tell me what they mean to you. If you tell me what they mean to you, you have to be right."

> "Here we go. *Close* and *near*."

"They are the same."

"Good. How about *apple* and *peach*?"

"They are the same and different. "

"How could that be?"

"They are both fruit but different kinds."

"Okay, good for you. *Couple* and *pair*."

"The same, but there might be a problem with that answer."

"How?"

"*Pair* to me means that the two things are related, like a pair of shoes or a pair of socks. In this case the two shoes or socks belong together. But *couple* could be two things that have no relationship at all. Like a couple of kids went swimming. But, sometimes a man and wife are called a couple, and they are related."

"Such excellent thinking on your part! *Money* and *pay*?"

"They are different, but not always."

"What?"

"Dad talks about getting his pay, and that is the same as money."

You can see the reader thinking here. With some practice, you both can learn a good deal about the relationships that some words can have.

Word Order

The order of words in an English sentence creates some of the meaning of the sentence. If the order of some words is changed, the meaning of the sentence changes. It will help your reader to get meaning from sentences if you do this exercise. You write/speak a sentence and have your reader change the placement of the words. See how many different ways the words can be put in the sentence and still have it make sense, as in the following example:

After dinner the spider ate the small fly.

1. After the spider dinner, the small fly ate.

2. The spider ate dinner after the small fly.

3. After the dinner, Small, the fly, ate Spider.

4. The spider ate the small fly after dinner.

5. The fly dinner the small spider ate after.

6. The spider ate after the small fly dinner.

7. The dinner ate spider after the small fly.

Another exercise having to do with order is one where only one word is changed. You create the sentence and your reader changes the order of the one word as many times as is possible but still must make sense with the sentence. The following example shows how to do this.

Only John went to the store.

John only went to the store.

John went only to the store.

John went to the only store.

John went to the store only.

John went to only the store.

Understanding the Elements of Fiction

Fiction can be interpreted through an understanding of each of the elements listed below. A thorough examination follows that will help your children derive meaning from any fiction.

I. **Setting**
   A. Time
   B. Place

II. **Characters**
   A. Actions
   B. Motives for acting as they do
   C. Relationships and how these affect their actions
   D. Speech
   E. Personality, the kinds of people they are (stingy, thoughtful, etc.) and how this affects their lives
   F. Weaknesses and strengths and what effect these have on how they function
   G. Physical characteristics and how these affect their behavior
   H. Intelligence and/or schooling and how these characteristics affect them in their relationships

III. **Conflict** — The problem of the story (the situation the characters face). Usually this takes the form of:
   A. Person against Person
   B. Person against Nature
   C. Person against Society
   D. Person against Self

IV. **Resolution** — Resolving of all the conflicts, both the main and those in any subplots.
   A. Establishing of what happens to the characters after the conflicts are resolved
   B. Explaining how the "problem" was understood and resolved (this is common in mystery stories and novels)

V. **Point of view**

   A. Person

   B. Tense

   C. Attitude

   D. Involvement

   E. Knowledge

   F. Perspective

Setting

The setting of a story consists of the time and the place in which a story occurs. Time includes season, or time of day, and place defines the location of the action. The initial setting is usually described in the first chapter because the factors involved in it help define the characters and conflict. It's not uncommon for the setting to change as characters face new experiences and changing circumstances. The establishment of the setting for stories or novels or for scenes in them are a major factor in creating the mood of the pieces. Mood in fiction is established by controlling the description of the following factors:

I.   Setting

    A. Colors and patterns

    B. The orientation and size of structures

    C. Lights and shadows

II.   Characters' attitudes toward place, situation, and other characters

III. Prior events

IV. Sentence length and variety

V.   Word choice

VI. Movement

VII. Dialogue

VIII. Narrator attitude

Understanding the Setting by Time

1. **Clothing style** — Indicates an approximate time-period, i.e., if the story takes place in "olden times" or in more modern times.

2. **Clothing type** — Indicates whether the characters live in the city or country, if they have money or are poor, how old they are, and whether they come from families who place importance on style or utility.

3. **Dialogue and language** — Reflect time periods by language styles, such as the use of "thee" and "thou."

4. **Machines and modes of transportation** — Indicate the time periods. Even very young children can get a feeling for the time of the story if horses are pictured pulling wagons or carriages. Modern cars, farm machines, and airplanes are good clues. Weapons also give good indications, i.e., guns, bows, swords, and clubs.

5. **Objects in the backgrounds of pictures** — Can indicate time periods if the objects are unique to a particular time. For example, houses, commercial buildings, or clock towers can, by their architecture, indicate time periods.

Understanding the Setting by Place

1. **The topography or geology** — The way the neighborhood is contoured or the part of the country in which the story takes place (the location of the action). If a picture shows deciduous trees (those that lose their leaves each year), that indicates the action takes place in the northern part of the world. If the trees shown are palms or the plants are those that grow in areas that are warm all year, then the young reader will know that the action takes place in semitropical regions. In either case, the attitudes and actions of the characters would be influenced by the geography.

2. **The immediate setting** — Details concerning the lifestyles of the characters. If the story occurs on a farm, there would be differences in the children's lifestyles compared to lifestyles of children growing up in the city. For instance, the children on farms would likely be doing chores, like gathering eggs and milking cows, that the city children would not do.

3. **Character attitudes** — The way the characters act toward each other. If the action takes place downtown in stores, the adults would have different attitudes toward children who they might or might not know than would the children's parents or other neighborhood adults.

Characters

The characters are the people in the story. In children's books, the characters are sometimes animals or anything else that can take on a personality. For a reader to understand a story, the characters must be understood. For most children, the fun of reading depends on this understanding. If the reader cannot relate to a character or to the situation that character is in or if the reader does not care about these things, that reader will not enjoy the narrative. But when the reader becomes involved in the lives and situations of the characters, then this experience will be very satisfying.

When an author writes, there is the entire world that may be described. Of course, this would not make sense and would take forever, so an author selects that which is important to the story and chooses not to describe what is not important. By taking note of what the author has chosen to describe, a reader can concentrate on what the author feels is significant. If a character is presented in detail, then the author must want the reader to concentrate on that particular one. The things described may also be clues to something that will happen later in the story.

Everything an author writes about characters is designed to create a reaction in the reader to those characters. This often produces a reaction called character identification and is carefully orchestrated by an author so that readers can empathize with the predicaments and joys the character experiences. There are three methods a writer uses in this character identification process:

1. Creating a character who is very similar to the intended readership (audience) so that the readers will recognize that they are like the character

2. Creating a character whom the intended readership would like to be like

3. Creating a character whom the readers know so much about that they understand why the character acts and reacts as he or she does

Understanding Characters

A reader can gain an understanding of characters by examining:

I. **The roles they play in the story** — There are two types of roles for main characters in a story: the *protagonist* and the *antagonist*. These terms represent the characters or forces. The conflict of a story results from the struggle between these opposing forces.

    A. Protagonist — This character or force is the main character that wants something. The Greek prefix *pro* means to advance, *agonistes* is the word for someone going through a struggle or a challenge. Young readers might identify him as the "good guy."

    B. Antagonist — The character or force opposing the protagonist; the "bad guy." This is remembered because the word starts with ant, a variation of anti, the prefix meaning against. This is usually the side of the conflict with the bad guy or the bad force, like a "big bad wolf" or harsh weather or greed.

II. **Their personality characteristics** — An understanding of a character will occur when your reader examines its personality using the following guidelines:

    A. Actions — Fictional characters, if they are carefully made, are subject to the same weaknesses that real people have, and when they speak, they are just as likely to exaggerate or lie. Therefore, when we want to know about characters, we should be careful that we do not believe everything they say. We should examine what they do, just as in real-life we do more than just listen to people as they talk about themselves; we watch what they do to tell what they are like.

    B. Their motives — In well-written fiction, there are motives for the actions of the characters. Just as in life, fictional characters do not just do things; there are reasons. Actions can be easy to understand, but sometimes the motives behind them are hard to spot. There are two types of motives:

        1. Internal — These are feelings the character has, such as fear, hope, faith, greed, anxiety, or any feeling.

        2. External — Motives based on forces outside the character, such as nature, laws, or other characters.

    C. Relationships — All characters in fiction develop relationships, just as people in life do. The choices characters make are often dictated by how they feel about other characters. It is important for readers to understand these relationships that have been created, so the characters' actions will make sense and the reader will not be surprised by what choices are made. Some relationships are obvious to new readers, but some relationships are subtle. New readers should be taught how to think about characters' actions and to relate them to relationships. This is a complicated process and will take some practice.

    D. Ways of speaking — The way people (characters) talk reveals a great deal about them. A careful listener/reader can judge what part of the country a character comes from, the amount of education that character has, how much interest the character has in other people, and, in many cases, what motivates a character's actions. Young readers will need help for some time before they will be able to "read" a character's speech. Noticing what characters say about themselves and what other characters say about them is another indicator of what characters are like.

    E. Personality traits — This can determine their success with the problem of the story. The success of the protagonist in a story is, in a major way, dependent on the kinds of people involved.

    F. Weaknesses and strengths — When we deal with people, we should be aware of the ways they are strong and the ways they are weak. We then can make allowances for their weaknesses, and we can count on their strengths. The same conditions exist in fiction. It is important to try to recognize and understand the weaknesses and strengths of fictional characters.

G. Physical characteristics — If an author gives a character unusual characteristics, the reader should pay attention to that character and watch that character's actions. Such characters' actions are often influenced by this trait or are the result of them being conscious of their appearance. If an author makes all of the characters average in appearance or does not give physical descriptions of them at all, then they are not what the author wants the reader to concentrate on.

H. Intelligence and education — The better prepared people are to solve problems, the more likely they are to be able to do so. Authors decide on the intelligence and schooling of their characters before they introduce them to their readers. If an author does not know how smart one of the characters should be, there would be no way that author could control the abilities of that character.

Literary Terms Related to Characters

1. **Fully Developed Characters** — Have personalities that are distinctive and explained in detail and are called full-dimensional or rounded-out characters. The plot centers on them, and these are the characters we get to know well. They are motivated by realistic desires, experience a full range of emotions, and interact with other characters.

2. **Flat Characters** — These are the characters who are one-dimensional; that is, we only get to know one side of their personality. They are in the story to advance the plot. Usually these are minor characters' parents, siblings, or people in the neighborhood. Flat characters often fit stereotypes, and subplots are sometimes built around them.

3. **Dynamic Characters** — These are fully developed characters. They undergo changes in the narrative. Dynamic characters are always found in great pieces of literature.

4. **Static Characters** — Static characters do not change, and their personalities remain the same throughout the story.

5. **Characters as Foils** — Those who are placed in a story with personalities or traits opposite others to make strong contrasts. Foil is a jeweler's term for gem settings that are used to make precious stones look bright. An author can make traits in one character stand out by contrasting them with those of another. Characters used as foils can be developed, flat, static, or dynamic.

6. **Character Consistency** — This means staying within the range of the personality the author originally develops. We would not expect the strong hero of a story to suddenly change and become weak.

7. **Dialogue** — Conversation between two or more characters or a conversation one character might have when alone. For instance, this could be one between a woman and her conscience.

8. **Personification** — The presentation of an animal or an object as if it had human characteristics.

    "The sad sighing of the sea..."

Sample Objectives Related to Characters

The following objectives contain questions that might lead to a discussion with your reader.

1. **Identification with Characters** — Identifying the literary techniques that prompt sympathy or empathy and what the author has done to make the reader feel like or want to be like a character

or not to feel for a character and the position that character is in.

2. **Personalizing** — Stating what the reader might do in the same situation as a character in the story. This might follow a brief discussion of what the character does in the situation. "That girl gives her balloon to that little boy who does not have one. I wonder why she does that. If you had been that little girl, would you have given him your balloon? If you were in a park and saw a little girl who had a balloon, would you want her to give you her balloon?"

3. **Character Analysis** — Choosing a character from the reading and listing the actions of that character, then evaluating if the character's words match the character's actions. "How does Mary treat her friend?" or "Would you like to have a friend like her?" or "Why?" or "Why not?"

4. **Motive Analysis** — Asking the child to talk about the actions of a character and then asking the child to explain why the character does those things. This is hard, and you both will need to practice this. "When it is time for the family to get in the car and follow the moving van out of the driveway and to go to their new house, what does Janet do?" (She hid.) "That was a strange thing to do. That would mean that the family would not be able to go. Why would she do that?" (So they could not leave.) "Why doesn't she want to leave?" (She would miss her friends.) "What does this tell us about how she feels about her friends?"

5. **Recall of Comparisons** — Locating or identifying likenesses and differences among characters, places, or events that are compared by the author. This will show an understanding of characters as foils.

6. **Recall of Character Traits** — Identifying or locating statements about characters that help to point out the types of people they are.

7. **Inferring Cause and Effect Relationships** — Guessing about the motives of characters and their interactions with others and identifying situations where actions caused or affected consequences.

8. **Inferring Character Traits** — Guessing about the nature of characters based on clues presented in the reading.

Conflict

Characters in stories will always have conflicts. There is an old saying, "If there isn't a problem, there isn't a story." Conflicts are the forces in a story acting against each other. Before writing, a writer decides about the nature of the conflict in the story, what the forces in the conflict will be, and what each character's involvement will be in it.

There will always be two "sides" of conflict or forces or characters in a story: the **protagonist**, who may be the hero or main character, and the **antagonist**, who is the force or character working against the protagonist. Young readers may simply define these sides as "good" and "bad."

For the conflict to create suspense, the strengths of the two sides of the conflict must not be in favor of the protagonist. The protagonist must overcome great odds and trick or outwit very powerful opposing forces or characters to be successful or to get what they want. This explains why the heroes in children's stories are very often alone or do not have adults (parents) to help them.

Understanding Conflict

I. **Nature of the forces** — This will determine the type of conflict that takes place. It will be either internal or external conflict.

A. Internal conflict — This is a conflict that takes place within a character, such as a guilty conscience. The reader must focus on the character with this problem and what the character's desires are (the protagonist force) and the opposition (the antagonist force) that is trying to keep those desires from being satisfied.

B. External conflict — A conflict that is between a character and some outside force, such as nature. For a reader to make sense of a story, both the character and the outside force must be understood. The reader must focus on these two forces as the external antagonist force tries to defeat the desires of the protagonist character.

II. **Situation** — There are four types of conflict which the protagonist may face: against person, against nature, against society, or against self.

A. Person against Person — In many stories the conflict is between two of the main characters, the protagonist and the antagonist. In this type of conflict, these two forces are made up of one or more characters who are pitted against each other. In stories for young children, a conflict of this nature might arise because the two characters want the same thing, such as a bike, a best friend, a video game, or parental attention.

B. Person against Nature — In a person-against-nature conflict, one character (or group of children or animals) has a struggle with elements of nature. Many adventure stories are written with this major conflict. This often is the ocean, the cold of winter, a storm, flood, fire, or wind. The story of man's struggle against these large natural forces is fascinating, and young readers particularly enjoy these contests.

   For this type of conflict to be meaningful for a young reader, the nature of the natural force must be understood. Some writers assume that their readers will understand conditions such as hypothermia or dehydration or how easy it is to become disoriented in a forest, but this is not always the case. If the characteristics of the natural force are not explained in a story, it would be difficult for young readers to appreciate the story.

C. Person against Society — A popular conflict is with a person against a group of people who are in control. Often this group is called society, and it may be represented by school teachers and administrators, city government workers, neighborhood council members, the church leadership, or members of a club or organization.

   Young readers need to understand the dynamics of a group and the power that some groups have. In a person against society conflict, one character is in a struggle with a group to which that member belongs. This could be a person or animal who does not want to do what the group thinks is best or right to do. This character might want to build a clubhouse, start an animal hospital in the neighborhood, go swimming at night, or pick on an unfortunate neighbor.

D. Person against Self — Some stories are written so that the main character has what is called an internal conflict, one between two forces within a character. This will involve what we call "better judgment" or "conscience" or moral or religious training. The character wants to do something that is hard to resist or to accomplish something that is known to be wrong. Young readers need help with this type of conflict.

   A person against self-conflict might be with a desire to eat more than is healthy and the knowledge that this is not a good thing to do, a desire to have something even if it means to steal it and the knowledge that stealing is wrong, a feeling of guilt over something that has been done, a fear of doing something, or where a character must or must not do something.

III. **The progression of the plot** — Once the setting is established and the characters are introduced, the conflict begins to unfold through a series of events. In many stories, there are also subplots that often tie in with the main plot at some point and add interest and action. Although every story is different, the conflict format is usually consistent and will progress in a sequence that looks something like this:

A. Situation/Exposition — The forces in the story are defined.

B. Complication — Actions occur that trigger the conflict. This does not have to be a major move or an important event. Some small thing might set off the conflict. At this point the sides are drawn and the rules of the conflict are set.

C. Rising Action — The conflict gains momentum. Now the forces in conflict are unstoppable in their struggle. The forces (desires of the characters) take over the action and drive the story to its conclusion.

D. Climax — A crisis results in the climax, the point in the action at which it is possible to tell the outcome of the conflict. This is often the most exciting or interesting part of the story. One side must be seen to be in the position of the loser and one the winner.

E. Falling Action — After the climax there is a point where the building movement of the story subsides or slows, leading the reader to the final resolution.

F. Resolution — The conflict is resolved. One side must lose, and one side must win. The story wraps up loose ends and answers remaining questions.

IV. **Character traits that affect conflict**

A. The kinds of people they are affect their success with the problem of the story. The success of the protagonist in a story is dependent on the kinds of people involved. In many stories for young readers, the protagonists solve their problems by out-thinking the antagonists.

B. The intelligence and education of the characters determines how they solve problems. The better prepared people are to solve problems, the more likely they are to be able to do so. Authors decide on the intelligence and schooling of their characters before they introduce them to their readers. If an author does not know how smart a character should be, there would be no way that author could control the abilities of that character.

Sample Objectives Related to Conflict

1. **Identifying the major forces of conflict in the story** — These are the protagonist and antagonist forces. For young readers, using the terms "good guy" and "bad guy" might be helpful.

2. **Sequencing the steps of the conflict** — In doing this, older readers might use the correct literary terms, such as Situation/Exposition, Complication, Rising Action, Climax, Falling Action, and Resolution. Asking young readers what happened first, second, and so on might be easier for them to understand.

3. **Identifying foreshadowing** — Recognizing places that the author uses foreshadowing in a text.

4. **Forecasting (predicting)** — Asking the reader to tell what will happen next. These questions should be preceded by a short review of the immediate events up to that time. "All the kids come to the party except Janet. What do you think will be the reason for Janet's not going to the party?" or "The bear comes right into the camp and walks into the tent. Do you think that bear will find the food in the box?"

5. **Personalizing** — Describing what he or she might do if faced with the same problem.

6. **Identifying motives** — Determining the reasons behind the conflict and whether it was preventable.

7. **Recognizing cause and effect relationships** — Identifying cause and effect relationships that affect the conflict. "The girl's trouble starts when she climbs out of her bedroom window."

8. **Identifying plots and subplots** — Recognizing the parts of the plot progression (the sides of the conflict, inciting force, rising action, crisis, climax, and resolution). Reader might also identify the subplots in the story.

Resolution

Understanding the Resolution

After the conflict has reached its climatic point and the outcome of the struggle is apparent, there is a time of "falling action" and then the resolution. The resolution of a story is the consequence of the conflict climax. Generally, when the conflict is resolved, the story ends. What we call story resolution is that part of the story after the climax produces a winner and loser to the conflict. In this part of narration, all questions are answered, and subplots are resolved.

Literary Terms Related to Resolution

1. **Falling Action** — The conflict has lost momentum and the story is coming to its end.

2. **Denouement** — Older students might call this portion of the story the "denouement," a French word meaning "outcome or result." Young readers may call it the "ending" or "conclusion."

Sample Objectives Related to Resolution

1. **Examining the Resolution** — Discuss with your child the ending of the story. Explain to your child the idea that stories might end in lots of different ways and still be good stories. It stimulates a child to think creatively about what might have been.

2. **Foreshadowing and the Resolution** — Look again at the story and discuss the author's use of foreshadowing that hinted that things would end as they do.

Point of View

Point of view can be complicated, so some explanation may be needed. For your young reader, the terms first and third person and present and past tense are enough of a challenge and sufficient for understanding stories. Older readers can comprehend much more about the nature of the narrative voice. Below is a chart and an explanation of the choices an author has in creating a voice.

Older readers should understand all the point of view choices presented here since an author's selection of point of view is necessary to the understanding of any fiction.

You may have to work with this section many times before your children feel comfortable with it. You can come back to this section as often as needed.

Good writers should make at least the following selections before they begin to write. Good readers should recognize these elements.

Person	First	Second	Third
Person — number	Singular		Plural
Tense	Past	Present	Future
Attitude	Subjective		Objective
Involvement	Participant		Observer
Knowledge	Limited	Omniscient	Objective
Perspective	Restricted to personal view		Omnipresent overview

Definitions of Point of View Options

Person

First singular — The narrator refers to himself or herself through the use of the pronouns *I*, *my*, and *mine*.

First plural — The narrator refers to himself or herself as part of a group through the use of the pronouns *we*, *our*, and *ours*.

Second singular — The narrator refers directly to the reader as an individual through the use of the pronouns *you*, *your*, and *yours*.

Second plural — The narrator refers directly to the reader as part of a group through the use of the pronouns *you*, *your*, and *yours*.

Third singular — The narrator refers to one character at a time and talks about groups of people only in the sense of them being observed by one individual: He saw the flag. She saw the people in the parade. Often uses the pronouns *he*, *she*, *it*, *his*, *her*, *its*, *hers*.

Third plural — The narrator talks about a group of two or more people, often using the pronouns *they*, *their*, and *theirs*.

Tense

Past — The narrative voice talks about things that occurred in the past.

Present — The narrative voice refers to actions as if they were happening at the time he is telling about them.

Future — The narrative voice tells about things that will happen in the future.

Attitude

Objective — This voice shows no emotional involvement in the actions in the narration. It seems to have no attitude about the characters or what they do and assumes almost a scientific objectivity about the events.

Subjective — This voice cares about the characters and what they do and lets the reader know this by making comments indicating it has made value judgments.

Involvement

Participant — The narrative voice is one of the characters who takes a part in the events in either a main or supporting role.

Observer — The narrative voice watches the action from some removed vantage point. It is never a participator, rather a viewer of events.

Knowledge

Limited — The narrative voice is part of the action and can't know what is happening in other places or know what happens to other characters when it is not with them.

Omniscient — This voice has a wide range of possibilities. It can be in more than one mind and know what is happening in many places. It has an expanded view of the action.

Objective — This voice has a narrow view as if it were speaking from knowledge gained by looking at the action in the house next door.

Perspective

Restricted to personal view — The narrative voice assumes the position of a person in the story either as a participant or an observer. This view is limited to what a real person could see, hear, and know.

Omnipresent overview — The narrative voice must have some form of omniscience, for it can describe things in two places at one time and take the reader into the past and future and can show the reader the actions from any angle or from any vantage point it chooses.

Examples of Point of View Options

Person — First and Third, Singular and Plural

First person singular:	*I saw* the dog.
Third person singular:	*He saw* the dog.
First person plural:	*We saw* the dog.
Third person plural:	*They saw* the dog.

Tense — Past, Present, Future

First singular, past:	*I saw* the dog.
Third plural, past:	*They saw* the dog.
First singular, present:	*I see* the dog.
Third plural, present:	*They see* the dog.
First singular, future:	*I will see* the dog.
Third plural, future:	*They will see* the dog.

Attitude — Objective, Subjective

First person, singular, past, objective: I saw *the hungry dog.*

(Note that the narrative voice gives no indication of how it feels about seeing a hungry animal.)

Third person plural, future, subjective: They will see *the poor hungry dog.*

Involvement — Participant (central or peripheral), Observer (minimal or non-involved)

First person, singular, past, subjective, participant: I felt sorry for the poor, hungry dog when *I had to chase it away* from the door.

Third person, singular, past, objective, observer: *He watched the cook chase* the hungry dog away from the kitchen doorway.

First person, plural, past, subjective, observer: We held the door so the cook could chase away the poor, hungry dog.

Knowledge — Limited, Omniscient, and Objective

Third person, past, subjective, observer, omniscient:

It was a cruel thing that the boys should have to hold the door *when they felt so sorry* for the lonely and hungry dog that the cook, *who really hated all animals,* chased away from the back of the trash-filled alley.

First person, present, objective, observer, limited:

Opening the door for the cook, I see the hungry dog and *watch through the crack in the hinge line* as the cook throws a rock and chases it away.

First person plural, past, subjective, observer, objective:

From our room over the alley, we looked down on the back of the restaurant and there saw the two boys hold the door for the cruel cook, so he could throw stones at the poor dog.

Perspective — Omnipresent overview and Limited to personal view

Third person, past, objective, observer, omniscient, omnipresent overview:

The dog had been in the alley happily rooting in the garbage only a short time when the two not-very-bright boys opened the door, and the cook, who never had liked dogs, threw stones, and *the frightened dog ran down to the corner and into the alley in the next block where it found better pickings anyway.*

Sample Objectives Related to Point of View

Understanding the choices an author has in selecting the characteristics of his narrative voice does not involve memorizing the definitions of the choices. There are many exercises in the *Writing Strands* books that teach how to control point of view, and this should be sufficient training in this skill.

Students should understand the following things about point of view:

1. Tell others what choices an author has in creating a narrative voice and give examples of each one.

2. Identify in any passage of narration what choices the author has made for the narrative voice and explain how they can recognize them.

3. Identify in their own writing the point of view elements they have chosen to use.

4. Talk about the effect a chosen point of view has on a piece of narration.

Appendices

Spelling Rules

If you look up a word with your student and show the derivation of the word, (where they come from; Greek or Latin, whether its background is German or French or English) and the prefixes and suffixes that apply and the connotations of the word (how we feel), your student can become an expert in that word. If you have each child make cards with the word boldly printed on them and put the cards up on the end of their beds, on their mirrors, in the bathroom, at their places for dinner, they will become immersed in those words and never lose their correct spelling.

The above exercises and the following list of spelling rules should make good practical spellers of your students.

These rules have exceptions, but they are easily mastered. Once your students have learned these few rules, they should keep them from making the most common spelling errors; in addition, the rules will assist them in determining the spelling of unfamiliar words.

Write *ie* when the sound is long *e*, except after *c*.

> Examples: believe, field, niece, ceiling, receive, conceit
>
> Exceptions: seize, either, neither, weird

Write *ei* when the sound is not long *e*, especially when the sound is long *a*.

> Examples: freight, weight, reign, forfeit, height
>
> Exceptions: friend, mischief, conscience

Only one word ends in *-sede, - supersede*; all other words of similar sound end in *-cede*.

> Examples: precede, recede, secede, accede, concede

Adding Prefixes

A prefix is one or more letters or syllables added to the beginning of a word to change its meaning.

When a prefix is added to a word, the spelling of the word itself remains the same.

Examples:	dis + satisfy = dissatisfy	mis + spell = misspell
	in + numerable = innumerable	re + commend = recommend

Adding Suffixes

A suffix is one or more letters or syllables added to the end of a word to change its meaning.

When the suffixes *-ness* and *-ly* are added to a word, the spelling of the word itself is not changed.

> Examples: plain + ness = plainness
>
> casual + ly = casually

Exceptions: Words ending in y usually change the y to i before -ness and -ly; empty - emptiness; heavy -heaviness; busy -busily; ordinary -ordinarily. One-syllable adjectives ending in y generally do not change in spelling: dry - dryness; shy - shyly.

Drop the final *e* before a suffix beginning with a consonant.

Examples: truly, argument, acknowledgment, judgment

Exceptions: love + ly = lov*ely*   hope + ful = hope*ful*

place + ment = plac*ement*   care + less = car*eless*

With words ending in *y* preceded by a consonant change the *y* to *i* before any suffix not beginning with *i*.

Examples: accompany + ment = accompaniment

plenty + ful = plentiful

satisfy + es = satisfies

intensify + ing = intensifying

modify + ing = modifying

Double the final consonant before a suffix that begins with a vowel if both of the following conditions exist: 1) the word has only one syllable or is accented on the last syllable; 2) the word ends in a single consonant preceded by a single vowel.

Examples: swim + ing = swi*mm*ing (one-syllable word)

confer + ed = confe*rr*ed (accent on last syllable; single consonant and single vowel)

benefit + ed = benefited (accent not on last syllable)

confer + ence = conference (accent shifted; consonant not doubled)

Plural Nouns

1. **The regular way to form the plural of a noun is to add an *s*.**

Examples: dog, dogs   cat, cats   house, houses

2. **The plurals of some nouns are formed by adding *es*.**

Add *es* to form the plurals of nouns ending in *s, sh, ch, z,* and *x*. The *e* is necessary to make the plural forms pronounceable.

Examples: dress, dresses   box, boxes   sandwich, sandwiches

dish, dishes   waltz, waltzes   bus, buses

3. **The plurals of nouns ending in *y preceded by a consonant* are formed by changing the *y* to *i* and adding *es*.**

Examples: country, countries   fly, flies

forgery, forgeries   theory, theories

comedy, comedies   salary, salaries

4. **The plurals of nouns ending in *y preceded by a vowel* are formed by adding an *s*.**

Examples: boy, boys   journey, journeys

monkey, monkeys   toy, toys

tray, trays   buoy, buoys

5. **The plurals of most nouns ending in *f* or *fe* are formed by adding *s*. The plurals of some nouns ending in *f* or *fe* are formed by changing the *f* to *v* and adding *s* or *es*.**

Examples:

Add *s*:

gulf, gulfs	safe, safes
roof, roofs	kerchief, kerchiefs

Change *f* to *v* and add *s* or *es*:

leaf, leaves	wife, wives
shelf, shelves	knife, knives

6. **The plurals of some nouns ending in *o preceded by a vowel* are formed by adding *s*; the plurals of most nouns ending in *o preceded by a consonant* are formed by adding *es*.**

Examples: *o* following a vowel:

studio, studios	radio, radios

o following a consonant:

potato, potatoes	hero, heroes

Exceptions:

soprano, sopranos	solo, solos
piano, pianos	concerto, concertos

7. **The plurals of a few nouns are formed in irregular ways.**

Examples:

child, child*ren*	tooth, t*ee*th
goose, g*ee*se	woman, wom*e*n
mouse, mice	ox, ox*en*

8. **The plurals of compound nouns written as one word are formed by adding *s* or *es*.**

Examples:

spoonful, spoonfuls	cupful, cupfuls
leftover, leftovers	strongbox, strongboxes

9. **The plurals of compound nouns consisting of a noun plus a modifier are formed by making the modified word plural.**

The modified word is the one that tells what the entire compound word does, not what it is. The plural of notary public is *notaries public* (they are *notaries*, not *publics*); the plural of *mother-in- law* is *mothers-in-law* (they are *mothers*, not laws)

Examples:

runner-up, runners-up	editor in chief, editors in chief

10. **The plurals of a few compound nouns are formed in irregular ways.**

Examples:

drive-in, drive-ins	six-year-old, six-year-olds
stand-by, stand-bys	tie-up, tie-ups

11. **Some nouns are the same in the singular and the plural.**

Examples: sheep, deer, trout, salmon, Japanese, fowl

12. The plurals of numbers, letters, and signs are formed by adding an apostrophe and an *s*.

Examples: two *s's*   two *4's*

+'s   T's

Citing Basic Sources

Students will find various ways to cite sources depending on the subject matter and their teachers. These include Chicago Style, MLA (Modern Language Association), and APA (American Psychological Association). If a specific source method is required, these can be found online or in reference books at a local library. The following are basic ways to cite material from various sources.

For books:

Name of author (first name, then last name), name of book (in italics), edition (if necessary), city and state where published, name of publishing company, year of publication, page numbers quoted from, if used. Also, note punctuation. For example:

Ken Ham, *The Lie: Evolution* (Green Forest, AR: Master Books, 1987), p. 32.

If it is a book which is a collection of several authors it should read: Name of compiler or editor, name of book (in italics), name of chapter (optional), name of author of that chapter (optional), and then the rest of the publication information. For example:

Bodie Hodge and Roger Patterson, editors, *World Religions and Cults: Volume 1*, "Defending the Faith," by Dr. Kenneth Gentry (Green Forest, AR: Master Books, 2015), pp. 23–25.

For periodicals:

Name of author of article (first name, then last name); name of article (in quote marks); name of magazine (in italics); volume number if used; and date (in parentheses); and page number. Also, note punctuation. For example:

Andrew Snelling, "Is Noah's Ark on Mount Ararat?," *Answers Magazine* 12 (May-June 2017): p. 54.

For an Internet source:

"About Us," Master Books, accessed July 06, 2017, https://www.masterbooks.com/about.

Teaching Vocabulary with English Word Roots

English words are made of small, interchangeable parts. Those parts are primarily Greek and Latin root words. By studying roots in a language arts course, students prepare to unlock the meaning of words in any subject. For example, if a student knows that the root word *com* means *with/together*, then whether he knows the word or not, he has instant insight into the meaning of it. He has insight into the meaning of *commas, components, common denominators, communism,* and so on.

Teaching root words is as easy as playing simple card games. You may organize the roots any way you like. Go to another set of roots once the first group is mastered. Students may learn the roots over several years.

Start by writing each root word on an index card. (Let the students refer to a the root words sheet until they do not need it.):

- select a game,

- deal the cards,

- have the student review his cards and ask for a match to one of them.

- Once a student gets a match for a card, he has to "say a smart word" using that root. For example, if a student is playing Memory and draws the card, *bio,* he will try to find the card that says *life*. If he gets a match, he says a word using the word *bio*, such as *biography* or *biology.*

- If a student makes a mistake in naming the match to a card, simply say, "try again."

Here are three simple card games.

The Memory Game
Turn cards upside down.
A student draws a card.
The student tries to find a match for the card they have drawn.
If the student gets a match, he or she says a "smart word" using the root word.
The next student takes a turn.
The student with the most matches at the end of the game is the winner.

Go Smart!
If there are two or three students playing, deal each student seven cards.
If there are more than three, deal each student five cards.
Taking turns, each player asks for a match to go with a card in his hand.
If the student gets a match, he or she must say a "smart word" using that root word.
The student with the most matches at the end of the game is the winner.

Snatch
Deal all cards evenly between players, face down.
Turn over one card in the center, beginning a center stack, called "the Snatch stack."
Players each add a new card to the Snatch stack until students can make a match with a card in their stack and the card showing in the Snatch stack.
The one creating a match says a "smart word" using that root word.
The one creating the match takes the whole central stack of cards and adds them to the bottom of his or her own face-down stack.
The first player to lose all his or her cards is out.

Root Words

ab	away from	micro	small
ad	to/toward	mill	thousand
agon	contest/struggle	mis	wrong
al	pertinent/suited to	mit	send
an	without	mono	one
ante	before	non	not
anti	against	ob	against
anthrop	human	ocul	eye
aqua	water	omni	all
ary	pertaining	onym	name
astr/aster	star	ophthalm	eye
auto	self	ora	mouth
bene	good/well	para	beside
bi	two	pater/patr	father
biblio	book	ped	foot
bio	life	pend	hang
capit	head	penta	five
cardi	heart	per	through
cent	hundred	peri	around
chloro	green	philo	love
chron	time	phobia	fear of
cid	kill	phon	sound
circum	around	phos/phot	light
com/con/col	together	pneum	air/wind/breath
contra/contro	against	poly	many
corpor	body	port	carry
cracy/crat	rule/government	post	after
de	down/away from	pre	before
dis	separation/reversal	pro	before/forward
dynam	power	proto	first
escent	becoming/growing	quadr	four
ex	of/former	re	back/again
flect/flex	bend	retro	back
frater/fratr	brother	se	apart
fy	make	scope	aim/view
gen	kind	sed	remain
geo	earth	semi	half
graph/gram	write	soph	wisdom
hemi	half	sub	under
homo	same	super	above
hydra	water	syn	together
inter	between	tele	far/distant
intra	within	terr	earth
iso	equal	theo	God/god
ity	condition/ quality	thermos	heat
ject	throw	thesis	position/place
logos	word/study	trans	across
mania	madness for	tri	three
mater/matr	mother	uni	one
med	middle	ultra	beyond/excessive
meter	measure	un	not
		video/vision	see

Common Noun Suffixes:

-ancy	state of being
-dom	general condition or rank
-ency	a quality or state
-hood	state of being
-ness	state of original adjective
-ship	to shape
-tion	expression of action or state

Common Verb Suffixes:

-ate	show office or function
-en	to make
-fy	to cause or make

Common Adjective Suffixes:

-ful	full
-ish	somewhat like
-less	without
-ly	contraction of like

Commonly Confused Words

already — previously

I have *already* done my math.

all ready — all prepared

Are you *all ready* for the math test?

altar — a table or stand at which religious rites are performed

This is the *altar* used in the Communion service.

alter — to change

Do not *alter* your plans because of that.

altogether — entirely

Mother is *altogether* against moving.

all together — all things in one place

The cups and plates will be *all together*.

brake — a way to stop or slow down

The *brake* on your bike will stop you.

break — to come apart

Use this pencil but don't *break* it.

capital — money used to start a business; the seat of government

We have $200,000 *capital* to start the new business.

Lansing is the *capital* of Michigan.

capitol — office building where the government workers work

I work at the *capitol*.

coarse — rough; crude

The homespun shirt was *coarse* and rough.

course — path of action or passage or direction

I like the *course* of action you have chosen.

complement — something that completes or makes whole

The tomato sauce will *complement* the pasta dish nicely.

compliment — praise

Janet's work deserves a *compliment*.

des'ert — a dry area

When the *desert* is irrigated, things can grow.

desert' — to leave

Good soldiers don't *desert* their comrades.

dessert' — last thing eaten at a good meal

My favorite *dessert* is ice cream.

its — possessive form of it

Our family must sell *its* second car.

it's — contraction of *it is*

It's time for dinner.

lead — (present tense) *going first;* a metal used in pencils

We want you to *lead*.

The *lead* in the pencil is broken.

led — (past tense) of *lead*

Bob *led* the way.

loose — free; not tight

The jacket is a *loose* fit.

lose — pronounced (looz) *to misplace*

Do not *lose* this money.

miner — a mine worker

The *miner* went into the hole.

minor — under age; of little importance

Minors cannot vote.

It is of *minor* importance.

personal — individual; private

My *personal* view is that we should go.

personnel — group of people in the same company

Our company *personnel* would like that insurance plan.

plain — not fancy; flat land; clear

Plain clothes sometimes are best.

The *plain* stretched before the wagons.

Does this make things *plain* to you?

plane — flat surface; airplane; a tool

The flat part of the table is the *plane.*

The pilot got into the *plane.*

Use the *plane* to smooth the wood.

principal — head of a school; the most important of a group

The *principal* will talk to the students.

The *principal* reason is that I want to go.

principle — a reason for a rule or a basic truth

This computer chip works on a new *principle.*

quiet — still; silent

The hospital zone is a *quiet* zone.

quite — completely; very

He was *quite* done.

He is *quite* a hero.

route — road; way to go

The *route* was well marked.

rout — a disorganized military retreat

The retreat turned into a *rout.*

than — a comparison

John is bigger *than* Jim.

then — at that time

We ate. *Then* we did the dishes.

there — at that place

We will be *there* soon.

their — showing ownership

It will be *their* pool.

they're — (contraction) they are

They're the kids to get the job done.

to — direction; connection

Let's go *to* the lake.

It should be glued *to* that piece.

too — more than enough; also

I have eaten *too* much.

I want to go, *too.*

two — one + one

There are *two* boys who will help.

waist — mid part of the body

Put the tape around your *waist.*

waste — useless spending; material no longer of value

Do not *waste* your money on that book.

That leftover material is all *waste.*

weather — what it's like outside

What's the *weather* going to be?

whether — a choice or alternative

I don't know *whether* to go or not.

who's — (contraction) who is

It's John *who's* going.

whose — (possessive form of *who*)

Whose book is this?

your — (possessive form of *you*)

Is this book *your* book?

you're — (contraction of *you are*)

I hope *you're* feeling better.

Glossary of Selected Literary Terms

This glossary should serve as a quick guide to the literary terms covered in all levels of the Writing Strands series (Beginning, Intermediate, and Advanced). For students who wish to dive deeper into the world of literature, you may have need for a more exhaustive list. Many of these can be found online. An understanding of these terms and literary devices will help students understand more complicated material while giving them the tools to make their own writing more interesting.

Allegory — A story that has a plain or surface meaning and also a hidden meaning that uses characters or events to stand for an abstract idea or event. The *Pilgrim's Progress* is an example.

Alliteration — Repeating the same first letter in closely connected words. *Peter Piper picked a peck of pickled peppers* would be an example.

Allusion — Referring to another literary work, character, or event using an indirect reference. *Opening Pandora's box* is an example.

Ambiguity — An ambiguous statement may be taken in more than one way and should be rewritten so that the meaning is clear.

Anaphora — In anaphora, the same word or phrase is repeated at the beginning of every line. Psalm 29 would be an example.

Antagonist — A character who opposes the central or main character.

Assonance — When vowel sounds are repeated closely together. *The early bird gets the worm* is an example.

Characters — The people or animals representing the forces in conflict.

Cliché — An expression or phrase that is overused.

Climax — The greatest moment of tension in the story. The turning point of the story.

Complication — The initial event in the plot that leads to the main conflict of the story.

Conflict — The struggle(s) the main character(s) face in the story; can be internal or external.

Dialect — Speech typical of a specific locale.

Dialogue — Conversation between two or more characters or an internal conversation a character might have with himself.

Dynamic character — A character that changes internally due to the action of the story.

Exposition — Background information that helps the reader understand the characters and story events better.

Falling Action — Story events that follow the climax and lead to the resolution of the story.

Flashback — Interruption of the action to show an event that had occurred at an earlier time.

Flat character — A character whose character stays static or flat, regardless of what they experience in the story.

Foil — A character who is the opposite of another character.

Foreshadowing — Giving of clues (hints) of events that will happen in the future actions in the story.

Hyperbole — Using intentional exaggeration to make a point. *She has a smile a mile wide* would be an example.

Idiom — A word or phrase that has come to mean something other than the plain definition of the words. *Bite the bullet* is an example.

Imagery — A description that gives the reader a picture of the action or location.

Imagery — Describing a subject with words that appeal to one or more of the reader's senses. *Lips as sweet as candy* is an example.

Irony — The exact opposite of what you would expect to happen in a situation, or to be said in a conversation. Example: A pharmacist who would not take his medicine.

Literary Present Tense — The practice of using present tense verbs when writing about characters and events in a work of fiction. This is done because the action exists in the present moment for the characters.

Metaphor — A metaphor is a comparison between two things that makes the two seem equivalent. *All the world is a stage* is an example.

Metonymy — Substituting the name of something with a word that is associated with it. Calling a policeman "the law" would be an example.

Mood — This is how the story makes the reader feel about a subject.

Onomatopoeia — When words sound like the thing they are describing. Examples would be *bang, buzz, click, drip, splash*.

Parallelism — Structuring parts of a sentence similarly. *That's one small step for man, one giant leap for mankind* is an example.

Parody — The making fun of an author's writing by the copying and exaggerating of that author's writing characteristics.

Personification — The presentation of an animal or an object as if it had human characteristics.

Plot — The pattern or structure of a story.

Point of View — The perspective that the narrative voice takes in relating the events of a story.

Polysyndeton — Repeating a single conjunction (often but not always "and") throughout a line or passage, even if the word is not grammatically necessary. Haggai 1:11 is an example.

Protagonist — The central or main character of a story.

Pun — A play on words using words that sound alike but have different meanings, or words that have several different meanings.

Repetition — When words or groups of words are used to create rhythm or to highlight an idea. Psalm 122:7-8 is an example.

Resolution — The point at which the plot finally ends.

Rising Action — Story events that lead up to the climax of the story.

Satire — The making fun of the weaknesses in people, institutions, or situations by exaggeration of their characteristics.

Setting — When and where a story takes place.

Simile — A direct comparison between two things using the words like or as. *As light as a feather* is an example.

Symbolism — The using of a concrete object (like a flag) to represent an abstract concept (like a country).

Synecdoche — Using the word for a part of something to describe the whole, or vice versa. *Lend me a hand* is an example.

Tone — In fiction, this is the narrator's attitude toward the text. In nonfiction, this is the writer's attitude.

*Glossary of Grammar Terms

Grammar, like so many other things in life, is a matter of terminology. If you want to master grammar, you will need to know the language of grammar. It is the same with math, medicine, music, finance, and so forth. The following terms are roughly alphabetical. That means under certain terms you will find other related terms.

Adjective — Its function is to describe or modify a noun. Adjectives have three forms of degree: positive (simple 1), comparative (*-ER 2*), and superlative (*-EST 3+*).

    Adjective Subject Complement — complements the subject; it describes the subject but is found in the predicate.

Adverb — Adverbs generally modify a verb; they give additional information about the verb according to TIME (when), MANNER (how), or PLACE (where).

Agreement — This is between the subject and the verb; their respective forms must agree with one another. For instance, ONE BOY RUNS, but MANY BOYS RUN.

Antecedent — the word (noun) for which the pronoun stands. In order, it comes before its substitute.

Apostrophe — an apostrophe is a mark to indicate possession or contraction.

Appositive — a noun or a pronoun acting as a noun that follows another noun to explain or rename it.

Baseword — Also **Headword**, it is the word which serves as the focus for other words in a group.

Cluster — a group of words all centering around a baseword.

Comma — a punctuation mark that represents a separation of ideas.

Comma Splice — When two halves of a compound sentence are joined/separated by a comma without a coordinating conjunction.

Complex Sentence — a sentence containing two independent clauses.

Compound Sentence — two complete sentences joined by a comma and a conjunction.

Conjunctions — Connectors, words used to connect two ideas together. This text identifies three types of conjunctions used in the addition method of sentence combining.

    Conjunctive Adverb — a weak connector requiring punctuation on both sides; common c/a's are *however, nevertheless, therefore, hence.*

    Coordinating Conjunction — connectors of any two equal grammatical units; the FANBOYS: *for, and, nor, but, or, yet, so.*

    Subordinating Conjunction — a word that joins two thoughts together but makes one dependent on the other; common subs are *if, when, although, as, because.*

Dependent Clause — a clause that cannot stand by itself; it is not a complete sentence.

Fragment — a sentence part lacking a subject or a verb, or both.

Gerund — see VERBAL.

Independent Clause — Complete sentence, a grammatical unit consisting of subject and predicate that makes complete sense in itself. See SENTENCE.

Indirect Object — the receiver of the direct object.

Infinitive — see VERBAL.

Intensifiers — words that limit the range of an adjective or an adverb. They always occur with an adjective or an adverb, never alone. Some grammars label intensifiers as adverbs. The most common intensifier is *very*.

Modify — to limit or qualify, usually associated with adjectives and adverbs.

Noun — In English this type of word is used to give names to persons, places, and things. An easy way to remember a noun is to think of it as a namer.

    Common Noun — refers to any one of a class or group of beings or lifeless things or even the collection itself; also it can refer to a quality, action, condition, or general idea.

    Plural — the form of a noun that represents two or more.

    Proper Nouns — refer to a specific or particular individual or thing. They are always capitalized

    Singular — the form of a noun representing one item.

Noun Baseword — the main noun in a cluster of modifiers grouped around it.

Noun Cluster — the group of words that form around a noun baseword.

Noun Marker — a word that marks a noun; the three most common Noun Markers are *a, an,* and *the.*

Noun Subject Complement — complements the subject, it is a second name for the subject but is found in the predicate.

Object — also **Direct Object**, the receiver of the action (direct object).

Object Preposition — the last word in a prepositional phrase; it is almost always a noun.

Ordinal Numbers — Numbers that show a list or series, as in "first, second, third."

Paragraph — a sentence or group of sentences developing one idea or topic.

Parallelism — a concept that is linked to using grammatical constructions in series. The parallelism rule simply states that the various parts of the series must all have the same construction.

Participle — see VERBAL.

Passive — said of verbs and sentences, it changes the word order in sentences. See TRANSFORMATIONS.

Preposition — a function word or a structure word. It is used to glue other words together, usually two nouns. The preposition will show either a time or a space relationship. Most prepositions show a space relationship.

Prepositional Phrase — a group of words beginning with a preposition and ending with its object.

Pronouns — For this text, it is both the class of words that take the place of nouns, in which case we will simply call them nouns, and those that act as Noun Markers, also called pronominals or pronominal adjectives by some.

Case — shown by personal pronouns, there are three different cases, nominative or subject case, accusative or object case, possessive or genitive case.

Gender — shown by personal pronouns, there are three genders: masculine, feminine, and neuter.

Person — shown by personal pronouns, there are three persons: 1st person speaks, 2nd person is spoken to, and 3rd person is spoken about.

Redundancy — using different words to say the same thing.

Relative — The basic relatives are *who, whom, whose, which, that* (+ *whoever, whomever*). These words relate a clause to another noun in the sentence, usually previous to the clause.

Relative Pattern — also **Relative Clause**, a clause, usually beginning with a relative, which modifies a noun or once in a while stands for a noun.

Run-on Sentence — combining two or more sentences into one without appropriate punctuation.

Sentence — A basic sentence is a sentence that is simple, declarative, and in the active voice.

Predicate — comes second and is the telling part. It always contains a verb.

Subject — This is the naming part of the sentence. It comes first and contains either a noun or a word or phrase functioning as a noun.

Simple Subject — It is the noun baseword of the cluster serving as subject in a sentence.

Sentence Combining — either putting two or more sentences into one or ideas from other sentences into a new sentence.

Addition — In this method two sentences are combined by simply adding the one sentence to the other.

Embedding — In this method some part of the source sentence is extracted and placed or embedded into the consumer sentence.

Sibilant — letters making a hissing sound (*s, sh, ch, x, z*)

Suffix — a syllable added to the end of a word.

Inflectional — a change of form that alters meaning but not word type; shows some grammatical relationship: number, case, degree, etc.

Derivational — a change of form that alters both the meaning and the word type.

Syntax — word order, important in determining the relationships of words in English.

Test Frame — a sentence with a blank in it used to test words to see if they are a particular type of word. This test is most useful in eliminating word classes.

Transformations — sentences that have had their normal word order adjusted. Three types of common transformations exist: yes/no questions, *there* + *be* constructions, and passives.

Transitions — bridges in writing that tie words or sections together.

Verb — the telling words; they generally tell what the subject is doing except for linking verbs.

Active Verbs — all verbs that are not linking; they show action of some sort.

Auxiliary Verb — a verb that helps the main verb; generally modals and forms of *have* and *be*.

Intransitive Verb — a verb that does *not* carry action across to an object.

Irregular Verb — a verb that doesn't form its past forms regularly.

Linking Verb — also called state of being verb; there are only 12: *be, become, remain, look, appear, taste, sound, smell, feel, act, grow, seem.*

Modals — nine auxiliary verbs that show probability: *can, could, shall, should, will, would, may, might, must.*

Regular Verb — a verb which uses *-ED* for its past forms.

Verb Cluster — It is formed around a verb baseword (Vbw); this cluster always follows a very rigid order. The syntax formula is MODAL (+ simple) HAVE (+ en) BE (+ ing) Vbw.

Transitive Verb — a verb that carries the action across from the subject to an object.

Verb Baseword — the main verb in a cluster of verbs and other modifiers.

Verbal — a verb that retains some qualities of a verb but does the job of an adjective or a noun. It modifies or acts as a noun substitute. The three types are participles, gerunds, and infinitives.

Gerund — an *-ING* form of a verb which substitutes for a noun.

Infinitive — a *TO* + verb combination which either 1) substitutes for a noun or 2) modifies some part of the sentence.

Participle — an *-ING* or *-EN* form of a verb used as a modifier.

*From *Jensen's Grammar* by Master Books®

GENRES OF BIBLICAL LITERATURE

The Bible contains numerous types of literature, or "genres," each with its own writing style. While some books of the Bible could fit into more than one genre, the following chart categorizes them by their primary genre only. Understanding the genre helps us identify the main purpose and setting of the book. Even though these books were written a long time ago, it is important to remember that they can and should help us grow spiritually today. (2 Tim. 3:16-17)

Law: The first five books in the Bible that describe the foundation of the world and the beginnings of history. They contain God's promise to Abraham to make of his descendants a great nation by whom all the families of the earth will be blessed, as well as the laws given by God (through Moses) to the people of Israel.

Historical Narrative: Books in the Bible that describe historical events that happened in the Old and New Testaments. They primarily cover the history of the Jewish nation (Old Testament) and the history of the early Christian church (New Testament).

Poetry: Books that deal with important questions and issues of life, such as suffering, daily living, relationships, and the nature of God. Often written in a poetic style.

Prophecy: These books record God's messages to the people in the Old Testament as spoken through the individual prophets. In the Bible, a "prophet" was a person called to speak for God. They spoke the words God gave them. Sometimes the prophets predicted future events, and sometimes they addressed current issues and events.

Gospels: These are the eyewitness accounts of the life, death, and resurrection of Jesus.

Letters: Letters written to individual people or groups of people, each with a specific message or purpose. These letters have a style similar to letters we would write today, including a greeting, a body, and a closing.

OLD TESTAMENT

Law	Historical Narrative
Genesis	Joshua
Exodus	1 Samuel
Leviticus	2 Samuel
Numbers	Ezra
Deuteronomy	Judges
	1 Kings

Poetry	2 Kings
Job	Nehemiah
Ecclesiastes	Ruth
Psalms	1 Chronicles
Song of Solomon	2 Chronicles
Proverbs	Esther

Prophecy

Major Prophets	Minor Prophets	
Isaiah	Hosea	Nahum
Jeremiah	Joel	Habakkuk
Lamentations	Amos	Zephaniah
Ezekiel	Obadiah	Haggai
Daniel	Jonah	Zechariah
	Micah	Malachi

NEW TESTAMENT

Gospels	Historical Narrative
Matthew	Acts
Mark	
Luke	
John	

Letters	
Romans	Titus
1 Corinthians	Philemon
2 Corinthians	Hebrews
Galatians	James
Ephesians	1 Peter
Philippians	2 Peter
Colossians	1 John
1 Thessalonians	2 John
2 Thessalonians	3 John
1 Timothy	Jude
2 Timothy	Revelation

GENRES OF WRITTEN LITERATURE

Poetry: Stylistic writing that utilizes devices such as meter, rhythm, metaphor, and/or rhyme (among many others); to express feelings and ideas or to tell a story. Poetry has several subgenres, including but not limited to: **Narrative, Lyric, Epic, Dramatic, and Satire**.

Prose: Writing that follows a straightforward grammatical structure of complete sentences and paragraphs. It resembles everyday speech. Both fiction and nonfiction are subgenres.

Fiction: Writing that is based on imaginary characters and events. There are many subgenres of fiction including but not limited to:

Fantasy

Western

Romance

Science Fiction

Thriller

Mystery

Detective Story

Dystopia

Historical Fiction

Nonfiction: Writing based upon the lives, events, and/or ideas of real people. Subgenres include but are not limited to:

Autobiography

Biography

Commentary

Theology

Legal

True Crime

Diaries and Journals

Textbooks

Travel

Self-help

Newspapers

WRITING STRANDS
SCOPE AND SEQUENCE

Level	Skill Level/ Grade	Skills	Lesson Titles (Writing Categories)	Reading Analysis Skills
Beginning 1	Designed for students who are in 5th-8th grade.	Focuses on skills such as sentence variety, paragraphing, and writing narratives.	What Is It? (Adjectives); What We Did (Listing); Like a Reporter (Reporting); Good Deed Report (Pronouns & Paragraphing); My Day (Ordering Actions); Groups (Grouping & Variety); Smart Bird (Telling a Story); Sell It (Convincing); Interview (Dialogue); Dear Class Member (Letter Writing); I Helped (Personal Experience); What's It Like? (Comparisons); "Hi There" (Greeting Cards); Animals (Role Playing); Summer! (Imagination); Communication (Eye Contact/Meeting People)	Adam & Eve (Main Idea & Characters); Abraham & Isaac (Character's Actions); Jacob & Esau (Descriptions of Character Appearances); Joseph (Fully Developed Characters); Moses & Pharaoh (Protagonist & Antagonist); Gideon & the Angel (Cause & Effect in a Story); David & Goliath (Foils in a Story); Jonah (Personification in a Story); Ruth & Naomi, Esther, Nehemiah, Jesus Calling the Disciples, Jesus & the Blind Man (Drawing Conclusions in a Story); John the Baptist (Physical Appearance); Jesus Healing the Paralyzed Man (Drawing Conclusions Practice); Jesus, the Disciples, and the Little Children (Character Motivation); Crucifixion (Character Consistency); Paul's Conversion (Character Comparisons)
Beginning 2	Designed for students who have completed Writing Strands Beginning 1 or who are in 5th-8th grade.	Focuses on foundational skills, written exercises, and the overall writing process.	Following Directions (Basic); Sentence & Paragraph Control (Basic); Write & Rewrite a Sentence (Basic); Description of My Friend (Description); Writing About Thoughts and Feelings (Creative); What Did You Do Today? (Organization); Furniture (Organization); Out the Window (Description); A Very Short Story (Creative); My Room (Description); How People Move When They Talk (Description); Story Events (Organization); Point of View (Creative); Tell a Story (Creative)	Introduction to Setting; Setting as Place & Time; Setting & Culture; Setting & Plot; Setting & Characters; Integral Settings vs. Backdrop Settings; Searching for Setting Clues; Setting & Mood: Physical Descriptions, Previous Events, Character Attitudes; Setting & Symbolism; Setting as Antagonist; Using Setting Clues to Understand the Culture, Character Actions/Attitudes/Motivation; Reviewing Setting

Level	Skill Level/Grade	Skills	Lesson Titles (Writing Categories)	Reading Analysis Skills
Intermediate 1	Designed for students who have completed Writing Strands Beginning 2 or who are in 5th-9th grade.	Focuses on skills such as organization, description, and paragraphing.	How a Sentence Does It (Basic); Connections (Organization); The Main Points (Organization); I Feel (Description); My Mistake (Organization); Narrative Voice (Creative); Controlling Point of View (Basic); Changing Tenses (Basic); Past, Present, and Future (Basic); Paragraphs (Basic); My Home (Description); Describing a Thought Problem (Organization); Things Change (Description); From Where I Was (Creative); Attitude in Description (Description); The Long and Short of It (Creative)	Plot in Literature; Story Plot & Sequence of Events; Cause & Effect in Plot; Character & Plot; Driving Forces in Plot; Elements of Plot: Exposition, Complication, Rising Action, Climax, Falling Action, Resolution, Putting It All Together; Plot: Conflict with Individuals/Society/Setting, Internal Conflict; Reviewing the Importance of Plot
Intermediate 2	Designed for students who have completed Writing Strands Intermediate 1 or who are in 5th-9th grade.	Focuses on skills such as organization, narration, and argumentation.	Narrative Voice Attitude (Basic); Interesting Sentences (Creative); Arguments That Win (Organizational); Write for Action (Basic); What the Narrator Knows (Creative); Narrative Voice Position (Descriptive); Where to Start (Organizational); Dialogue (Basic); Out of Time (Basic); My Thumb (Descriptive); Flashback (Organizational); Foreshadowing (Organizational); An Author Makes the Reader Feel (Creative); The New House (Creative); The Balloon (Creative); Writing Letters (Organizational); Communication (Classroom Techniques/Public Speaking)	Basic Literary Elements; Theme in Literature; Genre in Literature; Point of View - Limited, Objective, Omniscient; Dialogue in Literature; Point of View - Tense, First Person, Third Person; Tone in Literature; Mood in Literature; Point of View - Participant, Observer, Plural or Singular, Second Person

Level	Skill Level/Grade	Skills	Lesson Titles (Writing Categories)	Reading Analysis Skills
Advanced 1	Designed for students who have completed Writing Strands Intermediate 2 or who are in 9th-10th grade.	Focuses on advanced skills such as persuasive writing, reports, and developing characters.	Body Control (Creative); If I Were a… (Research & Report); Conflict (Creative); Point of View (Explanatory); Survey (Research & Report); Book Report (Research & Report); Customs (Research & Report); Interview with a Character (Research & Report); Who, Me? (Creative); Choices of Action (Creative); Problems (Creative); Writing Letters (Research & Report); Communication: How… (Conversation)	Intro to Literary Devices; Allusion; Imagery & Symbolism; Personification; Metaphor; Simile; Metonymy & Synecdoche; Puns & Wordplay; Irony; Hyperbole; Sonic Devices & Meter; Parallelism; Anaphora; Repetition; Polysyndeton; Reviewing Literary Devices
Advanced 2	Designed for students who have completed Writing Strands Advanced 1 or who are in 9th-10th grade.	Focuses on advanced skills such as research and writing, scientific reports, effective argumentation, and developing point of view.	What Our Feet Do (Creative); If I Were a… (Research & Report); Describing Characters (Creative); Conflict (Creative); Point of View (Explanatory); What Makes It What It Is (Creative); Survey (Research & Report); Argument (Argumentative); Book Report (Research & Report); Behavior (Research & Report); Interview with a Character (Creative); Problems (Creative); Interactions (Creative); He Did It First (Creative); Giving a Speech (Communication); Interviewing (Communication)	Pilgrim's Progress is read throughout the year; Genre in PP; Characters in PP; Setting in PP; Theme in PP; Plot in PP; Dialogue in PP; Point of View in PP; Imagery, Metaphor, and Simile in PP; Genre in PP 2; Characters in PP 2; Plot in PP 2; Setting in PP 2; Theme in PP 2; Tone and Mood in PP 2; Symbolism in PP 2; Writing a Literary Analysis Essay on PP; Write Your Own Allegory

Writing Strands

BEGINNING 1
GRADE 5-8

Students will master basic writing with unique exercises in dialogue, reporting, interviews, role playing, persuasion, story writing, organizing and grouping ideas.

BEGINNING 2
GRADE 5-8

Students will learn how to effectively master using sentences and paragraphs, main and supporting ideas, process of rewriting, point of view, and creating characters.

INTERMEDIATE 1
GRADE 6-9 *[1 YEAR / 1 CREDIT]*

Students will learn about effective paragraphs, descriptive writing, narrative voice, and tense usage, as well as how to analyze plots in literature.

INTERMEDIATE 2
GRADE 6-9 *[1 YEAR / 1 CREDIT]*

Students will study writing strong arguments, dialogue, papers, and letters, as well as literary elements like theme, genre, point of view, and tone.

ADVANCED 1
GRADE 7-10 *[1 YEAR / 1 CREDIT]*

Students will practice writing reports, short stories, essays, and other forms of writing and learn about literary devices, including imagery, symbolism, and rhetorical language.

ADVANCED 2
GRADE 7-10 *[1 YEAR / 1 CREDIT]*

Students will refine their writing and research skills and study John Bunyan's classic *Pilgrim's Progress* in-depth.

TEACHING COMPANION

Teachers will find this an invaluable resource, not only for using the *Writing Strands* curriculum but also for teaching any course that includes writing and literature as a component. The *Teaching Companion* provides a helpful overview of the *Writing Strands* system, as well as additional information on a range of writing, grammar, and literature issues that a teacher may face at any level of the program.

Available at MasterBooks.com & other places where fine books are sold.
800-999-3777